# THE REVENGER

*The Life and Times of Wild Bill Hickok*

## AARON WOODARD, PhD

**TWODOT®**

GUILFORD, CONNECTICUT
HELENA, MONTANA

**A · TWODOT® · BOOK**
An imprint of The Rowman & Littlefield Publishing Group, Inc.
4501 Forbes Blvd., Ste. 200
Lanham, MD 20706
www.rowman.com
A registered trademark of The Rowman & Littlefield Publishing Group, Inc.

Distributed by NATIONAL BOOK NETWORK

British Library Cataloguing in Publication Information available

**Library of Congress Cataloging-in-Publication Data available**

ISBN 978-1-4930-3392-8 (paperback)
ISBN 978-1-4930-3393-5 (e-book)

∞™ The paper used in this publication meets the minimum requirements of American National Standard for Information Sciences—Permanence of Paper for Printed Library Materials, ANSI/ NISO Z39.48-1992.

Printed in the United States of America

*To my mother, Gloria May Poling Woodard,*
*who always believes I can—period,*
*and to our family's newest arrival,*
*Olive May Tuinstra Boehler, my new grand-niece.*

*For rulers are not a terror to good works, but to the evil. Wilt thou then not be afraid of the power? Do that which is good and thou shalt have praise of the same . . . But if thou do that which is evil, be afraid; for he beareth not the sword in vain; for he is the minister of God, a revenger to execute wrath upon him that doeth evil.*

—ROMANS 13: 3-4 (KJV).

*There is no use in trying to override Wild Bill, the Marshal. His arrangements for policing the city are complete and attempts to kill police officers or in any way create disturbance, must result in loss of life on the part of the violators of the law.*

—ABILENE *CHRONICLE*, OCTOBER 12, 1871

# Contents

# Acknowledgments

Anyone who writes on Wild Bill Hickok must acknowledge the lifetime of scholarly work by the late Joseph Rosa. He scrounged documents and newspaper articles for years, enabling other researchers to piece together Hickok's life and death. I am especially appreciative for Rosa's dogged persistence to track down transcripts of McCall's second trial and the copies of petitions requesting a presidential pardon. Rosa did not have these available when he wrote his own biography of Hickok, and they were subsequently published in a later, much smaller book. This, then, is the first full-length biography of Wild Bill that contains the complete record of McCall's legal and political attempts to avoid the noose.

The professional library staff at the University of South Dakota's ID Weeks Library were also essential for their usual excellent and timely assistance. I especially appreciate Julie Junker at Circulation and the staff of the reference desk, as well as the professionals and students in the University Archives, who provided copies of very old magazine articles and pictures. They are true professionals, and I would stand them up against any library, anywhere.

Also, to my mom, Gloria Poling Woodard, for her constant encouragement.

And to the Lord, who makes it all possible.

# Preface: The Greatest
## of the Gunmen

Tales of outlaw gunmen from the history of the Old West are practically a dime a dozen. Men who infamously shot first and asked questions later were found all over the gold rush boom towns and cattle towns of the West. Most of the famous gunmen, and the lesser known too, were murderers, thieves, drunkards—you name it. Many of their gun battles arose from disagreements over things such as the attention of prostitutes, stolen horses, an insult or reproach, or any other trivial, yet deadly, event. However, one of the most famous of these—even famous in his own time—was the clearly different and remarkable Wild Bill Hickok.

Wild Bill Hickok is generally renowned as the greatest of these frontier gunmen, yet the vast majority of the violence he participated in was done in his official capacity as a lawman or in defense of himself or others. He was not a crook, a criminal, or a coward, unlike so many of his contemporaries. As George Armstrong Custer said of Hickok during his lifetime:

*He was a plainsmen in every sense of the word, yet unlike any other of his class. In person he was about six feet one in height, straight as the straightest of the warriors . . . Whether on foot or one horseback, he was one of the most perfect types of physical manhood I ever saw . . . Of his courage there could be no question; it had been brought to the test on too many occasions to admit of a doubt. His skill in the use of the rifle and pistol was unerring; while his deportment was exactly the opposite of what might be expected from a man of his surroundings. It was entirely free of bluster or bravado. He seldom spoke of himself unless requested to do so.*

*His conversation, strange to say, never bordered on the vulgar or blasphemous. His influence among the frontiersman was unbounded; his word was law, and many are the personal quarrels and disturbances which he has checked among his comrades by his simple announcement that "this has gone far enough," if need be followed by the ominous warning that when persisted in or renewed the quarreler "must settle it with me." Wild Bill was anything but a quarrelsome man; yet no one but himself can enumerate the many conflicts in which he has been engaged and which have almost invariably resulted in the death of his adversary . . . Yet in all of the many affairs of this kind in which Wild Bill has performed a part . . . there is not a single instance in which the verdict of twelve fair-minded men would not be pronounced in his favor.*[1]

Hickok's amazing abilities with firearms, his many extraordinary experiences, and the many reports of his generosity and regard for others merit a close and comprehensive analysis to determine the truth and history of this legendary lawman.

# Introduction

It was early fall 1871 in Abilene, Kansas, the famed Western cowtown that had been irrevocably transformed by the burgeoning American cattle industry that was growing out of Texas. Generally speaking, cattlemen were broke in the years immediately after the Civil War. Cash-poor Texans had found that as the Confederate cause had fled Texas, so had most of the liquid cash. In post–Civil War Texas a fully grown steer could be used to buy a fifty-pound bag of flour. Joseph McCoy, an entrepreneurial cattle buyer and speculator who could see profits where others saw obstacles, reasoned that if the droves of Texas longhorns could be shipped directly east to the waiting slaughterhouses and packing plants in places like Illinois, fortunes could be made.

Kansas stood between the vast herds in Texas and the packing plants of the North, however, and the state had legislation in place prohibiting Texas cattle from entering the state. The longhorns were known to carry a fatal contagion known as "Texas fever," so McCoy's first problem was convincing Kansas lawmakers and state leaders that a way could be found to isolate the longhorns from the Kansas cattle, thereby containing the spread of the pathogen. McCoy was able to finally purchase stock pens in the small town of Abilene, near the railroad tracks, which would make transport of the longhorns eastward remarkably easy, even though he was unimpressed with his first views of Abilene, "a small dead place, consisting of about one dozen log huts."[1] McCoy proved to be a tireless businessman and promoter. He was able to convince Kansas lawmakers that the longhorns could be safely delivered to Abilene through nonpopulated areas thereby lessening the fear of a Texas fever outbreak among the Kansas cattle.[2] The problem of convincing Kansas farmers and ranchers that it was safe for Texan cattle to pass near their land still remained,

Wild Bill with his famous ivory-handled Colt Navy pistols worn butts-forward, 1869.

however. Numerous Texas cattle outfits had tried the trip before and been set upon by border gangs, rustlers, gangs, and groups of enraged farmers, sometimes leading to armed confrontations between the trail-driving cowhands and their assailants. Undaunted, McCoy organized a traveling Wild West show that featured a giant steer and properly uniformed vaqueros and Texas cowboys to help promote his plans. His portable show went to St. Louis and Chicago (where some of the main markets for beef were located) and apparently won over most of his detractors.[3] Conveniently for McCoy, by the late 1860s Texas fever had begun to diminish naturally.[4]

His promoting, conniving, and showmanship worked—cattle poured into Abilene by the trainload. By the end of November 1867, more than one thousand railcar loads of beef had been driven to the stockyards outside of Abilene and shipped east for processing from the newly consecrated "city of the cattle kings."[5] One million head of cattle were shipped from Abilene in a five-year period after 1867.[6]

As a result Abilene experienced unprecedented growth, the "boomtown" phenomenon of Western legend. The previously sleepy village on the Kansas plains was inundated with a huge influx of cowboys, trail drivers, and cattle outfits. Along with this transient population came the inevitable businesses that catered to their rowdy clientele. Numerous saloons, gambling halls, and brothels, as well as dry grocers, hotels, dining halls, cleaners, doctors, merchants, and even a newspaper, the Abilene *Chronicle*, sprang up seemingly overnight.[7] The boisterous cowboys and those who preyed upon them with their commercial offerings were certain to eventually get out of control. The city government was in a precarious position. They wanted the cowboys and their dollars, but they did not want the resultant drunken gunfights, vandalism, and general mayhem that accompanied them. They needed law and order.

The lawmen who served in early Western towns were a diverse breed. Many had previously been gunmen themselves and had decided to hire out their services. For some, like the Earp brothers, keeping the peace was a sort of family business. One thing that is certain, however, is that being a sheriff or marshal in one of the boomtowns of the West was extremely dangerous. Combine large amounts of alcohol consumption, copious numbers of firearms, young men with plenty of cash to spend and very little in the way of personal boundaries to restrain them, and the stage is set for a tinderbox of violence that only awaits a small spark to erupt.

Lawmen, if they wanted to stay alive in such an environment, had to be as ruthless as their opposition. In other words, it was a very good idea to shoot first and ask questions later. Waiting, hesitating, considering, and contemplating were sure avenues to an early end to a promising law enforcement career, whether you ended up with a bullet in your heart or brain from a drunken lawbreaker. Police, marshals, or sheriffs were often faced with split-second decisions that meant the difference between life and death. The general feel that one gets from a perusal of period newspaper accounts was that most of the time, if an officer shot and killed an armed man in a scuffle, that was that. There was no public outrage. Most town councils, mayors, and policymakers were keen to remove the social riff-raff from their midst and to encourage outside investments, favorable newspaper coverage, business expansion, and the resultant increase in the tax base. And this attitude was by no means confined to the frontier of Kansas. As Dakota Territory rancher Theodore Roosevelt remarked in 1886 concerning his own confrontation with violent thieves, "They belonged to a class that always holds sway during the raw youth of a frontier community, and the putting down of which is the first step towards decent government."[8]

Thus it was, on the evening of October 5, 1871, that a tall, long-haired figure could be seen patrolling the streets of Abilene. He was considerably taller and had wider shoulders than was common for the average American male of the 1870s. Leander Richardson would later describe this imposing figure in *Scribner's Monthly*: "He was about six feet two inches in height, and very powerfully built; his face was intelligent, his hair blonde, and falling in long ringlets upon his shoulders; his eyes blue and pleasant, looked one straight in the face when he talked; and his lips, thin and compressed, were only partly hidden by a straw colored mustache."[9] It would have been easy for a casual onlooker who perhaps failed to recognize the figure's authority from his physical size to clearly see the two polished Colt Navy pistols worn butts-forward around the tall man's waist. Along with the pistols, he also sported a badge, identifying him as an enforcer of the law—in this case in the role of the town marshal.

He must have been a conspicuous sight that October evening in Abilene. By the order of the town council, he had already closed down many of the rowdier dens of iniquity in the town during his tenure, leaving a large number of unemployed, well-armed, and unhappy Texas cowboys within city limits. A shot rang out, though the Texans had been warned not to carry firearms within city limits. The tall lawman made his way toward the sound to investigate and was confronted by a large Texan named Phil Coe, who was backed up by perhaps as many as fifty Texas cowboys. Coe, who was armed, fired two shots at the marshal. Both shots missed. The marshal instantly opened fire and shot Coe twice in the stomach. Another armed man suddenly appeared at the edge of the marshal's sight and Marshal Wild Bill Hickok fired again, and inadvertently shot and killed his own good friend and deputy, Mike Williams.[10] As we will see, this was an unusual occurrence—Wild Bill rarely made a mistake with his aim or his shooting.

# Chapter 1

# The Beginnings

The future famed gunman, "Wild Bill," was born James Butler Hickok, in the small town of Tory Grove, Illinois, in May 1837.[1] His parents, who hailed originally from Vermont and New York, had relocated to Illinois in 1834, first to Putnam County then two years later to La Salle County.[2] Illinois, at that time, was considered a frontier state. There were hostile Indians and all the accompanying vicissitudes of a frontier family's life, including the unpredictable weather, which could vary from drought to flood, occasional prairie fires that laid waste to entire areas, and blizzards that could render visibility to zero and make even routine farm chores life-threatening.

Young Bill, however, seemed to be enamored with the romantic side of pioneer life, including the written exploits of famed frontiersman Kit Carson and others. Carson had become a household name back in the 1840s due to his famed role in the John C. Frémont's expeditions through the American West that resulted in the opening of the Oregon Trail. Frémont published his report on the expedition's findings in 1845 to national adulation—the *Southern Literary Messenger* declared that the report would "survive as long as the Sierra Nevada."[3] Frémont even named some landmarks after his friends including Carson River and Carson Pass. Bill was undoubtedly familiar with the internationally famed Carson and was later known to have owned a copy of Carson's biography, as well as another volume titled *The Trapper's Guide*. He was engrossed with the exploits described in these tomes and went so far as to tell his family members that one day he would beat anything Carson ever did or attempted.[4]

In his early teenage years, Bill developed a fondness and aptitude for the instruments that would come to define his life—firearms. His first weapon was likely a small single-shot flintlock pistol, in quite poor condition. He began a diligent pattern of marksmanship and hunting with this weapon, using it for hunting and frequent target practice. As he progressed to his later teenage years, with his father's assistance, he was able to upgrade his shooting irons to a better pistol and then a rifle, which allowed him a far greater range in his hunting (the difference in possible range between a pistol and a long-arm is quite significant). Area settlers were frequently bothered by the depredations of packs of roving wolves that would pick off calves, lambs, chickens, and whatever prey was available.[5] Bounties were offered for the deaths of these opportunistic predators, and young Bill eagerly obliged, using his new rifle and growing proficiency with firearms to kill these pests and then skin them and turn their coats in for the money.[6]

While Bill was moving through the years of his early youth and young manhood, the United States itself was moving toward a conflagration so great that some wondered if the nation would survive. In the years leading up to the Civil War, the many differences between the North and the South—including culture, economy, manners, habits, lifestyles, and values—were part of a chisel cleaving its way through the rock of the Union, but the greatest impediment to a peaceful continuance of national unity was the issue of slavery. Slavery had been an accepted part of the farm economy in the South since the beginning of the nation, and the South's investment in slaves was almost beyond comprehension. One current estimate holds that the total value of the slaves held in the South was greater than all the rest of the personal property combined—possibly worth as much as two billion dollars by 1860.[7] A prime field hand, a male slave who could be driven from dawn to dusk at unending labor in the cotton fields, would cost a plantation owner as much as $1,200.[8] By 1860 the number of slaves had ballooned to four million.[9] The slaves themselves had no rights whatsoever. Indeed one common way of increasing the slave population in the South was the frequent impregnation of female blacks by their masters, resulting in many mulatto slaves. Families were also frequently separated—mothers, fathers, and children all being sold to different planters.[10]

The nature of Southern agriculture gradually forced out smaller farmers and landowners and led to the increasing growth and power of a small but elite group of landowners who are sometimes referred to as "The Planter Class."[11] In 1850 this amounted to only 1,733 families that actually owned as many as one hundred slaves or more, but these were the wealthy elite who occupied Southern governorships, senate seats, and congressional delegations, and controlled the economy and society.[12] When the specter of emancipation appeared with the armed conflict of the Civil War, many poor whites were happy to risk their lives to hold on to their tenuous social position, one step up from the bottom.[13]

Attitudes about slavery in the Northern states were also complicated. More than one historian has posited that Southerners, who had frequent dealings with individual blacks at close quarters, liked individual blacks but despised the race, while Northerners tended to talk well of the Negro race in general, but when it came to dealings with individual blacks, they were just as racist as the Southerners they scorned. Abolitionists had high-minded ideals and morals, but freed blacks themselves were often feared and discriminated against in the North by blue collar workers, especially recent immigrants, who saw free blacks as competition for employment. They also feared the release of the millions of enslaved blacks in the South for the same reasons.[14]

Even the "Great Emancipator," Abraham Lincoln, was clouded by uncertainty and indecision on the issue of slavery as late as 1862:

*If there would be those who would not save the Union unless they could at the same time save Slavery, I do not agree with them. If there be those who would not save the Union unless they could at the same time destroy Slavery, I do not agree with them. My paramount object in this struggle is to save the Union, and it not either to save or destroy Slavery. If I could save the Union without freeing any slave, I would do it; if I could save it by freeing all the slaves I would do it; and if I could save it by freeing some and leaving others alone,*

*I would do that. What I do about Slavery and the colored race, I do because I believe it helps to save this Union; . . . I shall do less whenever I shall believe that what I am doing hurts the cause and I shall do more whenever I shall believe doing more will help the cause.*[15]

It would have been nearly impossible for any literate, moderately intelligent American in the late 1850s to not have taken a position on the topic of slavery. Despite any ambivalence that was felt in either the North or the South, abolition was the moral driver behind the North's cause and the symbolic representation of the vast divide between the economies and cultures of the North and the South. The intensity of this conflict was escalating to the boiling point at the same time that young Hickok left home for the first time and headed west for adventure and his famous future. And his first move would take him directly into the hotbed of violence that was growing between pro- and anti-slavery forces in Kansas.

## CHAPTER 2

# Bleeding Kansas

HICKOK LEFT HIS ILLINOIS HOME IN 1855 SEEKING ADVENTURE AND experiences and also to emulate an older brother, Oliver, who had left for California in 1851. He made his way to St. Louis, Missouri, boarded the steamboat *Imperial*, and headed west for Leavenworth, in the newly created Kansas Territory.[1] As tensions between the North and the South intensified, Kansas became the epicenter of the struggle between pro- and anti-slavery forces. Murderous bands of pro- and anti-slavery guerillas roamed the countryside and enforced their version of righteousness with gun, fire, and sword. Numerous atrocities were committed on both sides. The bloody struggles in Kansas generated by this contest of ideas were so violent that the Kansas territory had become known as "Bleeding Kansas."

This had been fueled by the completely misguided policy known as "Popular Sovereignty," a policy invented by Lincoln's rival for the US Senate from Illinois, Senator Stephen Douglas. Douglas was an important figure in pre–Civil War politics in America, at one time a very real presidential possibility, and was known for his booming oratory, earning him the sobriquet "The Little Giant" (he was only about four feet tall). Douglas, who probably hoped the idea would settle down the violence and generate investment and business expansion in the West (he was heavily invested in real estate in Chicago and in railroads and stood to make a fortune if Western settlement bloomed into Kansas), misjudged the fierceness of the hate on both sides. Pro-slavers from Missouri poured into Kansas as well as anti-slavery settlers financed by abolitionist forces.[2] The stage was set for confrontations, massacres, and legendary violence.

Young Bill Hickok allied himself with the pro-Union/anti-slavery forces when he arrived in Kansas. He became a member of a group of anti-slavery militia known as the "Red Legs," led by Jim Lane, a pro-Union man from Indiana. Lane was probably drawn to Kansas for the same reasons many others came: It was the center of action in the fight against slavery and for free soil.

Hickok proved himself to be a valued member of the group. He duly impressed all who saw him with his proficiency with firearms, as related by one of his earliest biographers, J. W. Buel:

> *A few days after his enlistment the regiment was called out on the commons west of town for drill and rifle practice. The range was one hundred yards and the guns used were common squirrel rifles. In the contest of marksmanship James [Hickok] easily beat every other man in the command and indeed made such excellent scores that Lane personally complimented his accuracy in the most flattering words. While this little ceremony was being conducted, a crow chanced to fly overhead, and greatly elated at the distinction being shown him, James drew a pistol from his pocket and shot the bird, then carelessly replaced his weapon without remark as to the excellence of the shot. The crowd of men, however, set up a wild cheering, and for several minutes the confusion was so great that Lane could not make himself heard.*[3]

Many of the famed gunmen who emerged after the Civil War, such as the James boys, the Earp brothers, and Hickok, had experience in the bloody Civil War confrontations. It is certainly possible that their later violent careers were influenced by their exposure to guns, violence, and the cheapness of life that was a central feature of the Civil War.

Bill Hickok's own record of violence certainly indicates he had little remorse or regret concerning the men he killed. In fact one could argue that his very deadliness with firearms was directly related to his lack of remorse or reflection when it came to killing. If he was threatened or if he felt justified in the line of duty as a lawman, he would unhesitatingly draw his pistols and shoot to kill. This alone distinguished him from 98 percent of the rest of the population who would undoubtedly deliberate, agonize, and weigh the issues before resorting to violence. However, such deliberation in a gun battle would almost certainly lead to a quick death.

Hickok's quickness with pistols was frequently remarked upon, as well as his unerring accuracy, such as the following comments by Leander Richardson, who became acquainted with Hickok in Deadwood:

> *He was the most courteous man I had met on the plains. On the following day I asked to see him use a pistol, and he assented. At his request I tossed a tomato-can about 15 feet into the air, both his pistols being in his belt when it left my hand. He drew one of them and fired two bullets through the tin can before it struck the ground. Then he followed it along, firing as he went, until both weapons were empty. You have heard the expression "quick as lightning?" Well that will describe Wild Bill. He was noted all over the country for rapidity of motion, courage and certainty of aim.*[4]

Some historians question the accuracy of some of Hickok's alleged exploit with pistols (such as shooting dimes out of the air or uncorking bottles with shots from his Colts, and so on), and no doubt some of the accounts have been embellished in an effort to sell books, magazines, and so on.

What we do know for certain, however, is that in many, many confrontations with armed opponents, Wild Bill Hickok emerged without a scratch, while his assailants or adversaries were mortally wounded by Hickok's skill with his pistols. This cannot have been an accident. Period accounts of his accuracy and speed with his pistols, as well as his fearlessness in the face of a fight, must have a ring of truth. It is certainly possible for someone to be a dead-eye shot when firing at paper targets and bull's-eyes. It is something else again when a living, planning, thinking, armed opponent has decided to draw a firearm and try to kill you.[5] Greater exploits were to come.

In 1857 Hickok decided to obtain some of the excellent Kansas farmland then available. This was possible because of the Federal Preemption Act of September 4, 1841, which provided that, "Every person, being the head of the family, or widow, or single man over the age of twenty-one years and being a citizen of the United States, or having filed a declaration of intention to become a citizen, as required by the naturalization laws is authorized to enter at the Land Office one hundred and sixty acres of un-appropriated Government land by complying with the requirements of said act."[6]

Kansas was, at that time, believed to be one of the richest farming areas in the world. As one period traveler wrote:

> *Our sojourn on the plains impressed our party with a strong belief that Kansas, at no distant day, will be one of the richest garden spots on the continent . . . The whole surface of your land gentlemen, is one of wild beauty, ready to toss into the lap of every venturer upon it, a farm. The genius which rewards honest industry stands on the threshold of your State, with countless herds and golden sheaves. Smiling ready welcome to all new-comers, of whatever creed or clime.*[7]

Hickok filed a claim for 160 acres in Monticello Township, Johnson County, Kansas. It was there that he also held his first law enforcement job, probably prompted to do so because of his imposing size and skill with firearms, when he was elected constable.[8] He erected a dwelling on his new farmstead but fell victim to the violence of the place and time, when pro-slavery guerillas, operating out of Missouri, attacked Monticello and subsequently torched Hickok's homestead. He rebuilt, but it was later alleged that the same confederate supporters fired his home a second time.[9]

By the end of 1857, Hickok apparently decided that the humdrum day-to-day labors of farming were not for him. Perhaps he recalled his earlier promises to his family that he intended to "outdo" all the exploits he had read about in those early days of his youth. In any case, he left his homestead and began a job as a driver for the Overland Stage Company. Hickok's routes included driving between St. Joseph, Denver, and points in Kansas, Colorado, and Nebraska and even as far as Santa Fe, New Mexico, and Salt Lake City.[10]

# CHAPTER 3

# Overland

BEFORE WIDESPREAD RAIL TRAVEL BECAME FEASIBLE, STAGECOACHES were the principal means of transport both for goods and citizens in the western United States. The famous Concord stagecoaches, constructed in Concord, New Hampshire, by Lewis Downing and Stephen Abbot, became the national—and even international—standard for what a stagecoach should contain. The Concords were constructed for different passenger numbers, from coaches that could hold six people all the way up to larger models that could accommodate twelve riders. Stage drivers like Hickok had to know a great deal of horse-craft to be able to control their six huge horses that provided the "horsepower" for the whole operation. Mark Twain would later describe some of the skills (including being able to work while asleep) required for the job in his famous 1872 book *Roughing It*: "Overland drivers and conductors used to sit in their places and sleep thirty or forty minutes at a time, on good roads, while spinning along at a rate of eight or ten miles an hour. I saw them do it often. There was no danger about it; a sleeping man will seize the irons in time when the coach jolts. These men were hard worked, and it was not possible for them to stay awake all the time."[1]

Along with the drivers, passengers also endured all sorts of discomforts. Hickok was known particularly as a wild driver, and he had a reputation for delivering a thrilling ride. According to Hickok's biographer, J. W. Buel, he was famous for the way he approached the terminus at Santa Fe:

*The last stretch of road entering Santa Fe was a slight decline and over this Bill almost invariably turned the horses loose and gave them the lash. The big Concord coach would bound along like a wounded monster, lurching the passengers side to side, dishing up dyspeptics, phlegmatic and rollicking dispositions indiscriminately, and bowling into the town finally the centre of a dust bank and the object of excited interest to everyone in the ancient Mexican City.*[2]

In spite of his wild ways, Hickok made a good record for himself as a driver. His most famed stage driving adventure occurred in the fall of 1858, when an unspecified band of Indians—possibly Sioux or Cheyenne, as the Sweetwater River ran through their territory—staged a series of raids on the stage company. Various company posts were attacked, as were other properties owned by the stage and freight company Russell, Majors, and Waddell, who went on to start the famed Pony Express. One stagecoach was reportedly attacked and the driver and three passengers killed. The Indians also made off with a number of ponies, which stalled the mail-delivery business until other horses could be delivered.

After the depredations, the stage company chose Hickok as the leader of a raiding/rescue party that intended to retrieve the stolen ponies. Hickok and about fifty men left the stage station on September 29, tracking the Indians possibly along the Sweetwater River. It was discovered that the original thieves had been reinforced by another band of Indians, swelling their numbers to around one hundred. Hickok took the lead on the recovery raid and led his men into the Indian camp, instructing them to use only pistols. The group found the stolen horses in an unpicketed corral and were able to recover not only the stolen mounts, but added to their number about one hundred Indian ponies that they drove off with them.[3]

Hickok continued work with the Overland Stage Company until late 1858, when he was hired by another famed Western stage company, Russell, Majors, and Waddell. This company was about to begin its famous experiment in rapid overland mail delivery, the Pony Express, in 1860, but Hickok was considered too tall and heavy to be a rider, so he was assigned work as a wagon and stagecoach driver. This did not stop him from having some extraordinary adventures, however.

During his tenure with this new company, one of the most controversial incidents related in the Wild Bill legend occurred as he and his co-driver, Matt Farley, were making their way between Independence, Missouri, and Santa Fe, in what is now New Mexico. Biographers and historians, such as J. W. Buel and Frank Wilstach, have never been able to come to a concrete conclusion as to what exactly occurred, but as later Hickok biographer Joseph Rosa noted, "something happened."[4] Evidently, Hickok was traveling about two miles ahead of Farley, driving his team through the Socorro Range, when he came upon a mother bear with two cubs directly in the road ahead of his wagon.[5] Mother grizzlies are certainly known to be one of the most dangerous of animals, willing to fight to the death to protect their young if they feel the least bit threatened. According to legend, Hickok fired one his pistols at the bear, and the ball did not kill her, but merely enraged the animal.

After Hickok had fired at—and probably wounded—the bear, he experienced this animal's ferocity firsthand. The wounded animal charged him and stopped any chance he might have had to escape its wrath by climbing onto the top of his large cargo wagon. He managed to fire his second pistol at the animal and created another wounding shot, this time in the bear's left foreleg—but still he managed no killing blow. The bear then made directly for him and engaged him hand-to-hand. Hickok was, like most frontiersman of the day, also armed with a large Bowie-style knife. This he drew and began a deadly combat with one of North America's deadliest predators.[6]

He was able to open several wounds on the animal, but in the process, the bear tore into the muscles in his shoulder and crushed his left arm from the elbow. The bear also managed to rake its long and powerful claws across his chest and left cheek. Hickok was eventually pinned by the bear, but this position allowed him to use his knife and literally disembowel his enemy, reportedly causing the bear's feet to become entangled in her own intestines. The battle lasted for about thirty minutes and left a bloody spectacle on the ground around the battle site. When

Hickok's fellow wagon driver Farley finally caught up to his position, he found Wild Bill on the ground, dreadfully wounded and soaked in his own and the bear's blood. It had been a narrow thing. Farley took Hickok to Santa Fe, where he was able to come under the care of a doctor, Sam Jones, who had a good reputation as a frontier physician (this was by no means a common thing at this time). Jones was able to patch up Hickok's wounds so that after two months he was able to be transferred to Independence. He had been so severely wounded that it would be some three months before he could resume any work-related duties whatsoever.[7]

Some of the stories concerning this incident have no doubt been glamorized to make Hickok appear invincible and as a hero. However, most of the accounts of this episode agree generally on one thing— Hickok was in a mix-up with a grizzly bear and barely escaped with his life.

When Hickok was eventually able to return to light work duties, the company transferred him in 1861 to one of its stations along the Oregon Trail, Rock Creek Station in Nebraska Territory. The stage company, which ran its coaches between St. Joseph and Denver, used Rock Creek as a relay post and stabled around twenty-five horses there. Hickok's main job was to guard the horses, as there had been a great deal of thievery in the area.[8] It was a job that would go a long way to making Hickok a legend.

# CHAPTER 4

# The Making of a Legend— The McCanless Affair

ACCORDING TO THE TRADITIONAL, "ORTHODOX" VERSION OF THE STORY of Hickok's time at the Rock Creek Station in 1861, David McCanless or McCandles, was a leader of a gang of horse thieves who attacked Rock Creek Station in an attempt to run off the stage company's horses. Hickok allegedly barred himself in the small cabin or shanty that served as his quarters when this thieving gang burst in upon him. Upon this assault, Hickok reportedly first shot and killed McCandles, and when the others rushed into the cabin, he was able to shoot and kill three more men and stab several others with his knife. In the end, Hickok was reputed to have killed eight men in the incident (one dying the next day). This tale became a huge sensation, principally because of a February 1867 *Harper's* magazine article written by George Ward Nichols. The magazine article accomplished the period equivalent of an Internet story "going viral." Almost instantly, Hickok became a superstar. The trouble with the article and the story is that they are simply not believable.[1]

One of the great challenges for historians of any era is to determine the validity of historical occurrences based on comparing contemporary sources and other evidence. Often, the "accepted" version is just the story that has been told most often—as Abraham Lincoln famously said, "If it is history, it must be true." And historians are often faced with opposing or even contradictory historical accounts of a certain event. When unravelling the truth behind the McCanless shooting and Hickok's role

An almost-smiling Wild Bill, circa 1874. SOUTH DAKOTA STATE HISTORICAL SOCIETY

within it, it is best to begin with the standard account that thousands of magazine readers read when Nichols published his famous story. Nichols was generally willing to take Hickok's word as the truth, and probably put a few words in the Westerner's mouth, as well. Nichols wrote:

*"I don't like to talk about the McKandlas affair," said Bill, in answer to my question. "It gives me a queer shiver whenever I think of it and sometimes I dream about it and wake up in a cold sweat. You see this McKandlas was the captain of a gang of desperadoes, horse-thieves, murderers, regular cut-throats, who were the terror of everybody on the border, and who kept us in hot water whenever they were around. I knew them all in the mountains where they pretended to be trapping, but they were hiding from the hangman. Mkandless [sic] was the biggest scoundrel and bully of them all and was always bragging of what he could do. One day I beat him shooting at a mark and then threw him at the back-holt. And I didn't drop him as soft as you would a baby you may be sure. Well he got savage about it and swore he would have his revenge on me sometime . . . It was in '61, when I guided a detachment of cavalry who were coming in from Camp Floyd. We had nearly reached the Kansas line and were in South Nebraska when one afternoon I went out of camp to go to the cabin of an old friend of mine, a Mrs. Waltman. I took only one of my revolvers with me, for although the war had broke out I didn't think it necessary to carry both of my pistols, and in all ordinary scrimmages, one is better than a dozen, if you shoot straight . . . Well I rode up to Mrs. Waltman's, jumped off my horse and went into the cabin, which is like most of the cabins on the prairie, with only one room and that had two doors, one opening in the front and the other on a yard, like. 'How are you Mrs. Waltman?' I said feeling as jolly as you please. The minute she saw me she turned as white as a sheet and screamed: 'Is that you Bill? . . . They will kill you! Run! Run!' 'Who is going to kill me? There's two that can play that game.' 'It's Mkandlas and his gang. There's ten of them and you've no chance. They've just down the road to the corn shack. They came up here only five minutes ago. MKandless was dragging poor Parson Shipley on the ground with a lariat around his neck. The*

*preacher was most dead with choking and the horses stamping on him.
MKandless knows you are brining in that party of Yankee cavalry
and he swears he will cut your heart out . . . It's too late, they are coming up the lane.' While she was talking I remembered I had but one
revolver and a load gone out of that. On the table there was a horn
of powder and some little bars of lead. I poured some powder into the
empty chamber and rammed the lead after it by hammering the barrel
on the table, and had just capped the pistol when I heard MKandless
shout, 'There's that d-d Yank Wild Bill's hors; he's here and we'll skin
him alive.' If I had thought of running before it was too late now and
the house was my best hold—a sort of fortress, like. I never thought I
should leave that room alive . . . 'Surround hid house and give him
no quarter,' yelled Mkandless. When I heard that I felt as quiet and
cool as if I was going to church. I looked around the room and saw a
Hawkins rifle hanging over the bed. 'Is that loaded?' said I to Mrs.
Waltman. 'Yes,' she replied. She was so frightened that she couldn't
speak out loud. 'Are you sure?' said I, as I jumped to the bed and caught
it from its hooks. Although my eye did not leave the door, yet I could
see she nodded yes again. I put the revolver on the bed, and just then
MKandless poked his head inside the doorway, but jumped back when
he saw me with a rifle in my hand. 'Come in here you cowardly dog!' I
shouted. 'Come in here and fight me!' Mkandless was no coward, if he
was a bully. He jumped inside the room with his gun leveled to shoot;
but he was not quick enough. My rifle ball went through his heart.
He fell back outside the house, where he was found afterward, holding
tight to his rifle which had fallen over his head. His disappearance
was followed by a yell from his gang, and then there was dead silence.
I put down the rifle and took the revolver and I said to myself, 'Only
six shots and nine men to kill. Save your powder Bill for the death hug
is coming . . .' There was a few seconds of that awful stillness and then
the ruffians came rushing in at both doors. How wild they looked with
their red drunken faces and inflamed eyes shouting and cussing! But
I never aimed more deliberately in my life. One, two, three, four; and
four men fell dead. That didn't stop the rest. Two of them fired their
bird guns at me. And then I felt a sting run all over me. The room*

*was full of smoke. Two got in close to me, their eyes glaring out of the clouds. One I knocked down with my fist. 'You are out of the way for awhile,' I thought. The second I shot dead. The other three clutched me and crowded me onto the bed. I fought hard. I broke with my hand one man's arm. He had his fingers round my throat. Before I could get to my feet, I was struck across the breast with the stock of a rifle, and I felt the blood rushing out of my nose and mouth. Then I got ugly, and I remember that I got hold of a knife, and then it was all cloudy like, and I was wild, and I struck savage blow, following the devils up from one side to the other of the room and into the corners, striking and slashing until I knew that everyone was dead. All of a sudden it seemed as if my heart was on fire. I was bleeding everywhere. I rushed out to the well and drank from the bucket, and then tumbled down to a faint. . . ."*

"You must have been hurt almost to death," I said.

"*There were eleven buck-shot in me. I carry some of them now. I was cut in thirteen places. All of them had enough to have let the life out of a man. But that blessed Dr. Mills pulled me safe through it, after a bed siege of many a long week,*" said Wild Bill.[2]

To support the veracity of his story, Nichols cited two witnesses who came upon Hickok shortly after the battle, a Captain Kingsbury and Dr. Thomas Thorne. However, based on other evidence, Hickok's later biographer Frank Wilstach (writing in the 1920s and a fairly rigorous researcher) doubted the entirety of the story and did not believe that Wild Bill was even fired upon at Rock Creek.[3] Wilstach believed that the main portion of the story was made up by Kingsbury and that he was able to deceive subsequent biographers such as J. W. Buel, perhaps the most famed of Hickok's nineteenth-century biographers, and Nichols.

The controversy over what really happened at Rock Creek started early. About the time Wilstach published his biography of Wild Bill in 1926, there was a serious ongoing feud between the Kansas and Nebraska historical societies about who and what Wild Bill Hickok really was and what really happened at Rock Creek. The official documents of the Kansas State Historical Society on the subject claim that David McCanless was a person who delighted in "fallen women, horse racing, gambling, wrestling, boxing . . . dog fighting and drinking. He was what the mountaineers called a 'rough customer.'"[4] McCanless (the spelling used in their documents) had originally intended to head for the goldfields near Pikes Peak, but after hearing discouraging stories of failure from returning gold-seekers, he decided to set up a small way station at Rock Creek, Nebraska, on the Oregon Trail. McCanless purchased land from Newton Glen and set up a toll bridge over Rock Creek, which apparently turned a tidy profit for him.[5]

The Kansas State Historical Society claimed that McCanless was wholly deficient in moral character. Before heading west, he was already a married man, but apparently when he struck out he left his family behind, supposedly determined to call for them after he made good. However, once he was settled at Rock Creek, he began an affair with Sarah Shull, who was reportedly a celebrated beauty. McCanless's family eventually arrived, and the story was that McCanless set up his mistress Shull in one wing of his ranch house, with his legitimate wife and family in the other. When Hickok arrived at Rock Creek in 1861, McCanless had sold part of his property to Russell, Majors, and Waddell, who sent Hickok there on light duties after his purported fight with the grizzly. The Kansas Historical Society claims that it was Hickok's attentions to Shull that precipitated the conflagration at Rock Creek.

A conflicting view of the incident at Rock Creek, and an account supported by the Nebraska Historical Society (the "Nebraska Version" of this incident), comes from the eyewitness testimony of McCanless's son, Monroe, who allegedly saw the entire "fight" and disputed many of elements that portrayed Hickok as a hero. Monroe claimed that the entire dispute revolved around money. His father had, in fact, sold the land on which Russell, Majors, and Waddell had their way station, but the company, notoriously and almost constantly in the red, was delinquent in its payments to McCanless. They had hired H. Wellman and his wife to oversee the station and run affairs for the company, and the Wellmans were also on site at the time of the confrontation.

Monroe's account of the event would appear in *Forest and Stream* magazine in 1927:

*We all came to the station. Father and I stopped at the house and Woods and Gordon went on down to the barn. Father went to the door, the kitchen door and asked for Wellman. Mrs. Wellman came to the door and father asked her if Wellman was in the house and she said he was; father said "Tell him to come out," and she said, "What do you want with him?" Father said, "I want to settle with him." She said, "He'll not come out." And father said, "Send him out, or I will come in and drag him out." When father made the threat that he would come in and drag Wellman out, Jim Hickok stepped to the door and stood by Mrs. Wellman. Father looked him in the eye and said "Jim have we been friends all the time?" and Jim said "Yes." Father said "Will you hand me a drink of water?", and Jim turned around to the water bucket and brought a dipper of water and handed it to father, and as he did he saw something take place inside that was threatening or dangerous; he stepped quickly from the kitchen door and stepped up on the step and said, "Now Jim, if you have anything against me, come out and fight me fair." Just as he uttered these words, the gun cracked and he fell flat on his back; he raised himself up to almost a sitting position and took one last look at me and then fell back dead. Now Woods and Gordon heard the shot and came running up unarmed to the door and just then Jim appeared at the door with a Colt Navy Revolver. He shot two shots at Woods and Woods ran around the house to the north. Gordon broke and ran, but Jim came out of the door and shot two shots at him and wounded him. Just as Jim ran out of the door, Wellman came out with a hoe and ran after Woods and hit Woods on the head with the hoe and finished him. Wellman then came running around the house where I was standing and struck at me with the hoe and yelled out, "Let's kill them all!" I dodged the lick and ran; I outran him to the ravine south of the house and he stopped there. When I made my escape from Wellman, I ran three miles to the ranch and broke the news to mother, and one of our hands hitched up a team and took mother to the station. I was so exhausted with my getaway that I remained at the ranch. I went up to the station next morning; there was quite a crowd had gathered for 25 or 30 miles up and down the trail. The first thing I saw when I got near the station was a crowd of men burying Gordon; they had brought his remains from down the creek up near to the station and had dug a grave on the little knoll and put him in boots and all, wrapped in a blanket. They made a rude box for father and Woods and buried them in the same grave on the hill south of the station. Their bones lay there for 20 years then I moved them to Fairbury Cemetery, about 10 miles west of Rock Creek. After the killing, my uncle J. L. McCanless, organized a crowd over in Johnson County and came over and arrested Hickok, Wellman and Brink and took them before a Justice of the Peace at Beatrice and they had a preliminary hearing before old Pap Toole, an aged justice, and they were acquitted.*

*The county was not organized at the time and the trial was merely a sham trial. I lost track of Hickok after this and did not hear of him until 1870; he was then in Junction City Kansas, that summer. Next he was in Abilene, then Dodge City, then Denver, Cheyenne and Deadwood. If Jim Hickok ever killed a man that had an equal chance, I would like to have the evidence. My father was no killer, horse thief, or desperado.*[6]

There are some difficulties involved in Monroe's story, as well. Why were Hickok and the others acquitted so easily, and why didn't the uncle of Monroe, one J. L. McCanless, later a state senator in Colorado, pursue the matter further?[7] Wilstach discovered more evidence on the matter in a small book published locally in Nebraska in 1912, *Pioneer Tales of the Oregon Trail and Jefferson County Nebraska* written by Charles Dawson. Dawson was a peripheral participant in the Rock Creek affair, as he had at one time owned the land where the Rock Creek Station stood. Dawson also claims that the entire issue revolved around McCanless's mistress, Kate Shell (spelled incorrectly—she was the previously mentioned Sarah Shull). Wilstach decided to track her down and obtain eyewitness testimony. He was eventually able to do so, but "how she was found and by what means cannot be told without breaking confidences."[8]

Shell or Shull was ninety-three years old at the time Wilstach interviewed her, "a neat gray haired little woman, quick spoken with a mind of her own."[9] Wilstach said that even after more than half a century,

Shull remained tight-lipped on the Rock Creek affair, "the incident is an exceedingly painful remembrance to her. Inducing her to talk was like opening an oyster with a blade of grass." She did answer a few of the questions posed to her. She said that shooting was not about any debts and that McCanless did steal horses for the Confederate Army. She also claimed that she was not directly present at the time of the shooting but was about two miles away at her house. She also said that she believed that Hickok killed McCanless in self-defense. She also said that her reason for believing this was that the morning of the shooting she had heard McCanless say that "he was going to clean up on the people at the station." The absolute truth of the Rock Creek incident will most likely never be established unless new and unknown evidence somehow comes to light (a development that seems unlikely at this point).

It seems possible that no further efforts were made to pursue Hickok after the shooting, because the McCanless family did not want the true relations between McCanless and Shull to come out publicly at a trial. This would have been a large embarrassment to the extended family and the young Monroe, as well as painful for McCanless's wife. Ironically, if the McCanless family was intent on protecting their reputation, most of the written accounts of the Rock Creek affair in the aftermath spend a great deal of time in character assassination of McCanless. The issue of indebtedness was also a factor, but deadly violence would probably not have ensued if the issue had been merely financial. That said, Hickok's actions were hardly the heroic stuff that many writers have made of them. In fact, the Rock Creek incident is a rather sorry start for what became a famous and sometimes heroic career of law enforcement for Wild Bill Hickok.

## CHAPTER 5

# First Shots

IN JUNE 1861, AFTER THE INCIDENT AT ROCK CREEK, HICKOK BECAME more directly involved in the Civil War on the Union side. He gained a civilian appointment with Union General (and somewhat famous western explorer) John C. Frémont as a wagon master, a job that utilized his previous experience with the Overland Stage Company. Hickok's first assignment involved accompanying a wagon train carrying provisions from Kansas to Missouri. During the trip, the train was attacked by Confederate cavalry, which captured the Union wagons. Hickok managed to escape—after killing four enemy soldiers—and made it to Union-controlled Kansas City. After Union cavalry were successfully dispatched to recapture the train, Hickok took control again and escorted the wagons safely to their destination at Sedalia, Missouri.[1]

Later Hickok was transferred to the command of General Samuel Curtis, where he served until the end of the war. During his service with Curtis, Wild Bill served as a civilian sharpshooter—or sniper—at the battle of Pea Ridge in Arkansas. He reportedly killed as many as thirty-five enemy soldiers using a long-range rifle and shooting from cover. He also migrated to an even more dangerous role under Curtis's command, functioning as a spy for the Union, serving undercover as a Confederate. He first posed as a rebel in the Confederate cavalry under General Sterling Price, and later he posed as a Confederate guerilla in Kansas.[2]

One of Hickok's exploits as a Union spy involved challenging a fellow guerilla (who wasn't aware of Hickok's loyalties) to charge the Union lines with him. When the pair was near enough for shouts to be heard, Hickok identified himself to the Union pickets and shot his rebel companion dead, allowing Hickok to deliver some stolen Confederate dispatches into the hand of General Curtis.

Hickok was supposedly involved in other Civil War adventures as well, including some that were famously reported by George Ward Nichols in *Harper's Weekly*. If we are to believe Nichols's account of events, Hickok obtained his most famous horse from a Confederate soldier he killed. Nichols would dub the horse "Black Nell" and endowed it with the magical powers of a Pegasus and unicorn combined. Supposedly Hickok could entice the animal to lie on a billiard table at his command and it would lie down at his command to dodge bullets, and so on—all of which was duly illustrated in *Harper's*.[3] Nichols's article, which appeared in February 1867 in *Harper's New Monthly Magazine* was popular in the East, but it was roundly criticized in the towns and cities where the events supposedly took place. The Springfield, Missouri, newspaper, the *Patriot*, in its January 31, 1867, issue, was especially harsh in its attack on Nichols's work, "The equestrian scenes are purely imaginary. The extraordinary black mare, Nell (which was in fact a black stallion, blind in the right eye and a goer), wouldn't 'fall as if struck by a cannonball' when Hickok slowly waved his hands over her head with a circular motion . . . Nor did she ever jump upon the billiard table of the Lyon House at 'William's low whistle'; and if Bill had . . . mounted her in Ike Hoff's saloon and 'with one bound, lit in the middle of the street,' he would have got a severe fall in the doorway of the barroom . . ."[4]

After the Civil War concluded, Hickok may have spent some time in territory that was set aside for Indians and may have had a relationship with a Sioux Indian named Mary Logan. Hickok had supposedly befriended her brother during the war, and afterward was invited to spend some time with the tribe, located near the Niobrara River, where he met her. The relationship was characterized as "chaste" by Hickok biographer J. W. Buel, who first mentioned it in his book, *Heroes of the Plains*, which may or may not be true. After Hickok's sojourn in Indian Territory ended, he emerged in Springfield, Missouri, where he was known to frequent the gambling establishments and where Hickok's most famous gun duel would occur. In Springfield Hickok became acquainted with an ex-Confederate guerilla and spy named Dave Tutt. Tutt and Hickok's similar assignments during their wartime service, even though both were civilians, perhaps made them familiars.[5]

Hickok and Tutt were both voracious gamblers and frequented the many card games that were always available in Springfield. During one of these sessions, Tutt accused Hickok of welching on a previous debt—Tutt claimed it was forty dollars and Hickok claimed it was twenty-five. In any case, Tutt took Hickok's gold watch off the table where it had been placed as security for Hickok's bets during the game. Tutt told Hickok that if he wanted his watch returned, he should meet him in Springfield's public square the next day at nine in the morning. Hickok is said to have replied, "You'll never get across that place with my watch unless dead men can walk."[6]

When the next day dawned, many who had been in attendance at the card game came to the public square at the appointed hour to see if anything would happen. Tutt appeared wearing Hickok's watch, and Hickok appeared on the other side of the square wearing his signature sidearms. Hickok warned Tutt not to move, but as he began to cross the square even after Hickok's warning, both men fired almost simultaneously. Tutt missed his man, but Hickok's aim was true and deadly. Dave Tutt was shot through the heart. This public encounter in the bright morning sunshine is probably the only well-known Western gunfight to have occurred in this fashion—nevertheless, the scenario became the standard for many Western movies and television shows, most of which were probably based on the Hickok–Tutt duel. The much more common scenario for a Western gunfight typically involved a gunman getting "the drop" on his opponent, as described by Theodore Roosevelt in his famous account of cowboy life on the Northern plains, *Ranch Life and the Hunting Trail*, published in 1888:

> *The "bad men" or professional fighters and man-killers are of a different stamp, quite a number of them being, according to their light, perfectly honest. These are the men who do most of the killing in frontier communities; yet it is a noteworthy fact that the men who are killed generally deserve their fate. These men are, of course, used*

*to brawling, and are not only sure shots, but, what is equally import-*
*ant, able to "draw" their weapons with marvelous quickness. They*
*think nothing whatever of murder and are the dread and terror of*
*their associates; yet they are chary of taking the life of a man in good*
*standing, and will often weaken and back down at once if confronted*
*fearlessly . . . others however will face any odds without flinching; and*
*I have known of these men fighting, when mortally wounded, with*
*a cool, ferocious despair that was terrible. As elsewhere, so here, very*
*quiet men are often those who in an emergency show themselves best*
*able to hold their own. These desperadoes always try to get "The drop"*
*on a foe—that is, to take him at a disadvantage before he can use his*
*own weapon. I have known more men killed in this way, when the*
*affair was wholly one-sided than I have known to be shot in a fair*
*fight; and I have known fully as many who were shot by accident. It*
*is wonderful, in the event of a street fight, how few bullets seem to hit*
*the men they are aimed at.*[7]

After the iconic shoot-out in Springfield, however, Hickok was
detained by the law and a trial was held, but it was determined that the
shooting was in self-defense. Eyewitness statements made before the
county coroner from the Greene County Archive in Springfield shed
some light on the events as they occurred. One man named Thomas
Hudson said that he saw Dave Tutt walk toward Hickok from the
courthouse while Hickok walked toward Tutt from the other side of the
square. Hudson said that he saw Tutt draw his pistol, but that he turned
away at that moment and couldn't verify what else was happening in
the square. Another man, named W. S. Riggs, testified as to the events
of the card game the previous night that precipitated the duel. Riggs
said that Tutt claimed Hickok owed him thirty-five dollars (Riggs said
it was thirty-five dollars, while other witnesses said it was forty—in any
case, money was owed), while Hickok disputed this and said the correct
amount was twenty-five dollars. Riggs verified that Tutt had kept Wild
Bill's watch as collateral until Hickok paid him the alleged debt. Riggs
had also witnessed the events on the square, and he claimed that Hickok
attempted to engage Tutt in conversation to make a settlement over the

watch. Riggs also claimed that he saw Tutt pull his pistol and fire at Hickok first, but since Hickok was not facing him, he could not be sure who fired first. He testified that he heard two shots and then saw Tutt run around one of the pillars of the courthouse before collapsing, mortally wounded. Riggs would also state that he believed the distance between Tutt and Hickok was about one hundred yards.

A man named Eli Armstrong was also on the square, and he verified to the court that the issue was a dispute over the amount Wild Bill allegedly owed to Tutt. He also gave some background on the Hickok–Tutt relationship, saying that Hickok and Tutt had always been able to resolve their differences in the past. Armstrong reported that Wild Bill was heard to say to Tutt, ". . . you have accommodated me more than any man in town for I have borrowed money from you time and again and we have never had any dispute before in our settlement." Armstrong also verified that Hickok warned Tutt not to cross the public square wearing Hickok's watch. He said that, "Tutt made no reply but placed his hand on the butt of his Revolver. Tutt fired and so did Hickok but witness could not tell which fired first. Tutt then turned round and placed his hand on his breast and said boys I am killed and ran into the courthouse and fell at the door and rolled out on the ground at the door and died in about two minutes and perhaps not so long. Saw a bullet hole in his right side is satisfied both fired."[8]

Two important pieces of the Wild Bill myth fall into place due to the story of this iconic shoot-out. The eyewitness testimony would indicate that Hickok's shot entered Tutt from the side and that Tutt must have been facing Hickok but standing sideways. Hickok's mark was not only about one hundred yards away, but it was also half the size of a man facing him directly. He truly was a deadly marksman.[9] The second piece of the creation of the Wild Bill myth falls into place when studying the major discrepancies between the famous account of the Tutt–Hickok fight written by Nichols in his extensive 1867 article in *Harper's* and the witness statements. Apparently Tutt and Hickok were not known to be enemies. In fact, it was alleged by one man in Springfield, Colonel Albert Barnitz, that "they had been intimate for years and have been gambling together today. The ill will seems to have originated at the gambling table."[10]

In Nichols's exaggerated version of the tale, there were years of bad blood between Tutt and Hickok. The dramatic scenes painted by Nichols in his *Harper's New Monthly Magazine* article describe the duel in vivid, unverifiable detail, "The instant Bill fired, without waiting to see if he had Tutt, he wheeled on his heels and pointed his pistol at Tutt's friends, who had already drawn their weapons. 'Aren't you satisfied gentlemen?' cried Bill, as cool as an alligator. 'Put up your shootin-irons or there'll be more dead men here.' And they put them up and said it was a fair fight."[11]

There is also no eyewitness testimony that substantiates Nichols's version of events, which at least served to glamorize the shoot-out and sell magazines! But in addition to the lack of witness corroboration, Nichols was certainly an excellent dramatist, if not a good historian, and there are a number of things wrong with Nichols's account. Foremost, no gunman alive (especially not Hickok) would have whirled around before making sure his enemy was incapacitated. He would have waited with a

Cowboys on a cattle drive, 1870s. Wild Bill would confront men like these during his years as marshal. SOUTH DAKOTA STATE HISTORICAL SOCIETY

keen eye on his opponent to make sure a second shot was not needed. Perhaps Hickok was very fortunate that he made a killing shot, thus silencing any opportunity for Tutt to speak for himself or to leave his version of events for historians. We are left with Hickok's version of events, the coroner's witness statements, and Nichols's embroidery. All seem to point to a duel between reluctant participants over a relatively minimal debt, but that Hickok probably shot Tutt in the belief that his own life was in mortal danger, thus drawing a verdict of self-defense for Hickok.

Another substantial consequence of this duel for Hickok was a story that appeared in the July 27th *Missouri Weekly Patriot*, which is believed to be the first time Hickok is referred to in print as Wild Bill:[12]

> *David Tutt of Yellville Arkansas was shot on the public square, at 6 o'clock P.M. on Friday last, by James B. Hickok, better known in Southwest Missouri as "Wild Bill." The difficulty occurred from a game of cards. Hickok is a native of Homer, Lasalle county, Ill., and is about 26 years of age. He has been engaged since his 16th year with the exception of about two years, with Russell, Majors and Waddell, in Government service, as scout, guide or with exploring parties and has rendered most efficient and signal service to the Union cause . . ."*[13]

The public was not happy with the verdict of not guilty as recorded in the *Patriot* again:

> *The general dissatisfaction felt by the citizens of this place with the verdict in no way attaches to our able and efficient Circuit Attorney not to the court. It is universally conceded that the prosecution was conducted in an able, efficient and vigorous manner and that Colonel Fyan* [sic] *is entitled to much credit for the ability, earnestness and candor exhibited by him during the whole trial. He appeared to be a full match for the very able Counsel who conducted the defense . . . Those who severely censure the jury for what they regard as a disregard of their obligations to the public interest . . . should remember that they are partly to blame themselves. The citizens of this city were shocked and terrified at the idea that a man could arm himself*

Wild Bill, circa 1875. SOUTH DAKOTA STATE HISTORICAL SOCIETY

*and take a position at a corner of the public square, in the centre of the city, and await the approach of his victim for an hour or two, and then willingly engage in a conflict with him which resulted in instant death; and this too with the knowledge of several persons who seem to have posted themselves in safe places where they could see the tragedy enacted. But they failed to express the horor and disgust they felt, not from indifference, but from fear and timidity. Public opinion has much to do with the administration of justice and when those whose sense of justice and respect for law should prompt them to speak out and control public sentiment, fail to do so, we think they should not complain of others. That the defendant engaged in the fight willingly it seems is not disputed, and lawyers say . . . that he was not entitled to an acquittal on the ground of self-defense unless he was anxious to avoid the fight, and used all reasonable means to do so; but the jury seems to have thought differently.*[14]

## CHAPTER 6

# From Gambler to Marshal

IN FEBRUARY 1866, AFTER HIS ADVENTURES IN SPRINGFIELD, HICKOK moved along to Fort Riley, Kansas, where, upon the strength of his reputation as a wartime scout (and his deadly prowess demonstrated against Dave Tutt), he was appointed deputy US marshal. Hickok spent a good deal of his time at the fort maintaining peace and quiet. In those post-war years, tensions were high between the soldiers and the civilian laborers and scouts. Evidently Hickok was generally able to subdue troublemakers without resorting to deadly violence through his size and stentorian voice and presence.[1] He also spent time in the field searching for deserters, as well as horse and timber thieves.[2] And he was attached as a scout to various army cavalry detachments, including one commanded by the famed General William Tecumseh Sherman.[3]

From 1867–1869, Hickok interspersed his service as a lawman with freelance scouting work for the US Cavalry. He was engaged as a scout for General Winfield Scott Hancock's 10th Cavalry force in Kansas that had been dispatched in an effort to make peace between the government and the Cheyenne and Kiowas. As a scout, Hickok carried dispatches, serving as the army's mobile communications man. It was certainly dangerous and risky, but Hickok seemed to enjoy risk-taking and chancy actions.[4]

Inflated accounts of Hickok's alleged exploits were beginning to give him a fearsome reputation, particularly the 1867 article in *Harper's New Monthly Magazine* by George Ward Nichols. Most of these stories were probably outright falsehoods or highly exaggerated, but nevertheless they led Hickok into a continuing series of adventures that only increased his profile. In May 1869, the former vice president and US senator from Massachusetts, Henry Wilson, requested that Hickok serve as his guide for his western trip. Wilson was an unusual politician, as he did not come from wealth. His father was a foreign laborer, and he himself engaged in a variety of jobs including apprentice farmer and shoemaker. Prior to the Civil War, he was a well-known anti-slavery advocate and served as a noted member of the Free Soil Party. He is also generally credited with being one of the organizers of the Republican Party.[5] It was fairly common during this period and later in the nineteenth century for wealthy Easterners or even foreign visitors to seek out the services of a well-known Western guide for a tour of the famous American West. Hickok agreed to serve as a guide for the senator's entourage for the princely sum of one hundred dollars per week.[6]

The expedition lasted for five weeks, during which Hickok proved an interesting and capable wilderness guide. The pampered senator and his family were shown various sites where famous massacres and killings had occurred, as well as live bison. After the excursion was complete, Wilson gave a dinner for Hickok, at which time he supposedly presented him with a pair of ivory-handled Colt 1851 revolvers, which despite much investigation by firearms enthusiasts, have thus far been untraceable.[7]

Hickok next showed up in Hays City, Kansas, in 1869. He had spent some time in the rough frontier town earlier and had supposedly escorted Wilson's party through the town during their frontier adventures. (The Kansas newspapers do not mention the party visiting Hays City, so—as with so many things—it may or may not be true.)[8] He had also visited the town earlier in his capacity as a deputy US marshal, as noted in a local newspaper:

*W. F. Cody, government detective and Wm. Haycock [sic]—Wild Bill—deputy US marshal, brought eleven prisoners and lodged them in our calaboose on Monday last. These prisoners belonged to a band of robbers having their headquarters on the Solomon and near Trinidad and were headed by one Major Smith, once connected with the Kansas 7th. They are charged with stealing and secreting government prop-*

*erty and desertion from the army. Seventeen men, belonging to this same band, were captured eleven miles from Trinidad on the 13th of March, and sent to Denver, Colorado Territory for trial."*[9]

A passing traveler next mentioned Hickok's presence in Hays in August in another newspaper article: "Hays City, three hundred miles west of State Line, is the present live town of the plains. The first man we saw was 'Wild Bill.' He was ready, waiting to give welcome to the excursionists. Gentle William said he had brought two hundred of the nastiest, meanest Cheyennes to Hays that we might get a sight at the red men who did most of the murdering and scalping during the trouble of the past two years."[10]

Hays City was known as a tough frontier town. A former sheriff had been murdered in an ambush in 1867, and the general atmosphere was not conducive to peace and quiet.[11] The city served as the end of the line for the Kansas Pacific Railroad, and this made Hays City a prime shipping point for thousands of head of cattle from Texas. These herds were driven up the trail to Hays City by very tough Texas cowboys, who looked forward to arriving at trail's end and blowing off steam (and divesting themselves of their wages) at the more than one hundred gambling halls and brothels then extant in Hays.

The city had about two thousand permanent citizens in addition to the transient population. Along with the cowboys who brought the dust into town, Hays was also frequented by soldiers from Fort Hays, which was a short distance away from town.[12] About the only thing the cowboys and soldiers had in common was that they carried guns, used alcohol, and were usually interested in causing some sort of trouble or public disturbance when they came into town.

Hickok was involved in several major fracases in Hays City. His first major confrontation there occurred with a dangerous drifter known as Samuel Strawhun or Jack Strawhorn.[13] Strawhun was known about Hays as a violent man and was ordered out of the city by a vigilance committee that was trying to instill some law and order to the town. The town postal clerk and member of the vigilance committee, Alonzo Webster, told Strawhun and one of his companions, named Weiss, that they were no longer welcome in town, and things grew deadly. According to the *Junction City Union* of July 31, 1869:

> *A special from Hays City to the Leavenworth Commercial states that Joe Weiss, formerly of the Leavenworth penitentiary, and lately of the plains, was shot through the bowels Friday afternoon, by A. D. Webster. The affair occurred in the post office, in which Webster was a clerk and was a most justifiable act. Weiss, together with another ruffian named Strawhun, threatened Webster's life because he served upon them a notice to leave town, by order of the vigilance committee. They entered the post office about 3 P.M., abused, slapped and finally drew a revolver upon Webster who was too quick for them with the above result. Webster has been acquitted.*[14]

After the shooting, Strawhun left town but returned with friends undoubtedly with the plan of killing the postman. When Strawhun entered the post office, however, he instead found Wild Bill at the postal counter, who told them he would take over the fight if needed.[15] "Let them come," he supposedly said when he took the job of stand-in for the clerk. "We are ready for them," he added, patting his twin 1851 Colt Navies.[16] Hays's lack of a full-time law enforcement officer was not working, and a representative of the law was definitely needed. The townspeople had learned in their attempt to organize a vigilance committee that they needed someone with a reputation and a gun, such as Hickok, to back them up. After the Weiss and Strawhun incident, the citizens were hoping that a new sheriff would be appointed by Kansas's Governor James Harvey. Harvey demurred, however, because he did not believe he had the right to make such an appointment. It is somewhat uncertain as to the exact timeline, but the prominent citizens of the city apparently then turned to Hickok and asked him to assume the duties of town marshal.[17]

Hickok took office as sheriff of Ellis County on August 23, 1869.[18] The local newspapers discussed the beginning of Hickok's term thusly, ". . . contrary to current opinion, he 'Wild Bill,' was never the official sheriff of the town but had been appointed by a few citizens to act as marshal."[19] Miguel Otero, whose father was on the vigilance committee in Hays, wrote later that, "The Vigilance Committee showed discretion and sound judgment in securing as town marshal the famous 'Wild Bill' Hickok."[20] Hickok took the reins as law officer with both hands. One resident in Hays described Hickok's normal routine when he patrolled around town at night, noting that he carried a sawed off shotgun with both barrels cocked for action as well as two pistols, a pocket pistol, and a bowie knife.[21] He would stroll about the town, day and night, watching for trouble and discouraging it with his presence. According to the reminisces of an elderly citizen, Hickok had three rules for dealing with lawbreakers in Hays, "Law for persons considered dangerous to the community consisted of a choice of three things: 1. Take the first east bound train out of Hays, 2. Take the first west bound train out of Hays, 3. Or, go north in the morning. And North meant Boot Hill."[22]

One of Hickok's first fatal encounters after he assumed the official duties as law enforcement officer in Hays City was with a dangerous local ruffian named Bill Mulvey or Melvin on August 24, 1869. A local newspaper carried the following story on the incident, "Last night, Bill Hickok, better known as Wild Bill, acting Sheriff of Ellis County, while attempting to preserve peace among a party of intoxicated roughs or 'wolves' shot a man named Bill Melvin through the neck and lungs. Melvin is still living but doctors say with no hope of recovery. He attempted to shoot several citizens and was determined to quarrel with everyone he met, using his revolver freely but fortunately wounding no one."[23] During the later inquest, a witness gave testimony that Hickok had distracted Melvin before he shot him by looking over Melvin's shoulder and shouting, "Don't shoot him in the back, he's drunk," thus gaining a few precious seconds before Melvin could react.[24] It may seem "unsporting" if this is true, but one can imagine that gunmen, both lawmen and outlaw, scouted for every advantage in a gunfight, especially in a situation such as Hickok's, where he may have been facing more than one assailant.

Hickok was remembered as a ruthless lawman in several less-substantiated incidents. One local historian described a time when Hickok thought a prominent local businessman, Simon Motz, who had forgotten his keys, was trying to open a window to enter his business.

Supposedly Hickok saw him, believed him to be a burglar, and promptly clubbed him over the head with a board, knocking the man out cold.[25] Hickok was also alleged to have shown off his pistol-handling skills when he had some free time. One local man remembered, "I saw him draw his pistol in front of the old depot, throw it over his first finger, cocking it with his thumb as it came around and keep a tomato can jumping for a whole block down to old Riley's saloon on the next corner and it also took a good horseman to do a trick like that. He was not a drunken, quarrelsome man-killer, but picturesque and fine shot. It was not always the blustering bullies that were the bravest men in a western town."[26]

One of the more dangerous characters who Hickok confronted in Hays was a man named Jim Currie. Currie was dangerous because he was unpredictable. Once, when Hickok was sitting in a saloon, Currie managed to get behind him. The story went that:

*Currie slipped up behind and pressed his cocked revolver against his head saying, "Now you son of a gun! I've got you." Bill did not move a muscle. He showed no concern. He realized his danger but said in a casual way, "Jim, you would not murder a man without giving him a show?" Jim replied, "I'll give you the same show you would give me, you long-haired tough."*

*Everyone present knew the peril in which Bill stood, and the suspense was awful. Tommy Drum's oath was "By the boot!" He was running about the saloon in great perturbation exclaiming, "By the boot! By the boot!" Bill was really the only cool self-contained man in the room and remarked, "Jim, let us settle this feud. How would a bottle of champagne all around do?" The manner in which Bill had taken the whole incident, and the unconcern with which he made this remark relieved the tension and all burst out laughing. Tommy Drum opened a pint bottle of champagne for everyone present. Currie and Bill shook hands and the feud between them was over.[27]*

There is little doubt that Hickok's coolness and calm behavior saved his life in this instance.

However, there are many instances of local residents or travelers through Hays remembering that Wild Bill was not always so wild after all. Miguel Otero recalled that Hickok would often take him and his brother to hunt buffalo. According to Otero, he would help the two boys get a good shot at the animals. He also recalled that his parents never worried about them when they were in the care of Hickok.[28] One traveler, W. E. Webb, wrote extensively about Wild Bill as part of his account of passing through Hays:

*Monday was our day of final preparation, and we commenced it by making the acquaintance of those two celebrated characters, Wild Bill and Buffalo Bill, or more correctly, William Hickok and William Cody. The former was acting as sheriff of the town and the latter we engaged as our guide to the Saline. Wild Bill made his entrée into one court of the temple of fame some years since through* Harper's Magazine. *Since then his name has become a household word to residents along the Kansas frontier. We found him very quiet and gentlemanly, and not at all the reckless fellow we had supposed. His form won our admiration—the shoulders of a Hercules with the waist of a girl. Much has been written about Wild Bill that is pure fiction. I do not believe, for example, that he could hit a nickel across the street with a pistol-ball any more than an Indian could do so with an arrow. These feats belong to romance. Bill is wonderfully handy with his pistols however. He then carried two of them, and while we were at Hays snuffed a man's life out with one; but this was done in his capacity as an officer [probably Melvin]. Two row-dies devoted their energies to brewing a riot and defied arrest until, at Bill's first shot, one fell dead and the other threw up his arms in token of submission. During his lifetime Bill has probably killed his baker's dozen of men, but he has never, I believe, been known as the aggressor. To the people of Hays he was a valuable officer, making arrests when and where none other dare attempt it. His power lies in the wonderful quickness with which he draws a pistol and takes his aim. These first shots, however, cannot always last. "They that take the sword shall perish with the sword;" and living as he does by the pistol, Bill will certainly die by it, unless he abandons the frontier. Only a short time after we left Hays two soldiers attempted his life. Attacked unexpectedly, Bill was knocked down and the muzzle of a musket placed against his forehead, but before it could be discharged the ready pistol was drawn and the two soldiers fell down, one dead, the other badly wounded . . . The Professor took occasion, before parting with Wild William, to administer some excellent advice, urging him especially, if he wished to die in his bed, to abandon the pistol and seize upon the plow-share. His reputation as Union scout, guide for the Indian country and sheriff of frontier towns, our leaders said, was a sufficient competency of fame to justify his retirement upon it. In this opinion the public will certainly coincide.*[29]

Hickok consistently showed a remarkable combination of cool-headedness under extreme life-endangering stress, as well as the very quick reactions of a gunfighter, mingled with good judgment that enabled him to win gunfights, but not to be the aggressor. He killed, but his killing was done in his capacity as a law enforcement officer in the performance of his duties. He did not begin the fights—he ended them. He did have a national reputation, thanks to the greatly inflated claims of the 1867 *Harper's New Monthly Magazine* article by George Ward Nichols, and there were (and are) psychopaths and sociopaths with guns who were eager to test their mettle against a famed gunfighter and lawman like Wild Bill.

One story has Hickok almost ambushed and killed while he was rooming at a Mrs. John Mueller's at some point in his tenure in Hays. Hickok was about to leave the boardinghouse when Mrs. Mueller stopped him and warned him she had seen a man with a gun across the street who she thought was waiting to kill him. Hickok borrowed a coat and cap from the woman, pretended to have a limp, and slipped out wearing his disguise, passing right by the gunman.[30]

Perhaps the most dangerous encounter Wild Bill had during his time as a peace officer in Hays was his second run-in with a dangerous troublemaker named Sam Strawhun (or Strawhorn—various sources spell it various ways). The two met again on the night of September 27,

1869. Strawhun was causing a disturbance in a local tavern by demanding more beer and keeping the glasses, so the bar owner was running out of mugs. Hickok ordered Strawhun to cease and desist, but Strawhun tried to attack Wild Bill with a broken beer bottle. Hickok drew his pistol and shot Strawhun, killing him instantly. One newspaper reporter wrote that, "Sam Strawhim was shot and instantly killed by Wild Bill (J. B. Hickok), Sheriff, at one o'clock this morning . . . It appears that Strangham and a number of his companions being 'wolfing' all night, wished to conclude by cleaning out a beer saloon and breaking things generally. 'Wild Bill' was called upon to quiet them . . ."[31]

Another newspaper report described the incident as follows:

*It seems that there was on the part of this Stranhan [yet another spelling!] and some of his associates bad feeling against certain citizens of this town, and members of the vigilance committee. To satisfy their hatred they mobbed together and went on Sunday night, about half past 11 o'clock to the saloon of Mr. John Bitter, with the intent to break up the establishment. The crowd, numbering about fourteen to eighteen persons, called for beer in a frantic manner. The glasses had to filled up continually. Meanwhile the men were passing in and out of the saloon, and as it afterwards appeared carried the glasses to an adjoining vacant lot. Mr. Bitter remarked that the number of glasses was diminishing, and saw that Stranhan carried out some of them. The noise was fearful, all the men crying out at the top of their voices, beer! beer! And using the most obscene language. This went on for a short time, when they began throwing the beer at each other. During all the noise one could hear threats as, "I shall kill someone tonight just for luck," or "someone will have to go up tonight [to the cemetery]," etc. Mr. Bitter finally called the policeman, Mr. Wm. Hickok, known as Wild Bill, asking him to go out and fetch the missing glasses back. Wild Bill shortly returned with both hands full of glasses, when Strawhan remarked that he would shoot anyone that should try to interfere with his fun. Wild Bill set the glasses on the counter, Stranhan took hold of one and took it up in a threatening manner. He had no time to exercise his design for a shot fired by Mr. Hickok killed him. He dropped*

*down dead. The inquest was held next morning at nine o'clock. The
verdict of the jury was that deceased was shot by Mr. Hickok and that
the homicide was justifiable, the same being in self-defense. Too much
credit cannot be given to Wild Bill for his endeavor to rid this town
of such dangerous characters as this Stranham was.*[32]

More details were provided by other newspapers, where the shooting
was big news, "About twelve o'clock last night a difficulty occurred in
this place at the house of John Bittles between a party of roughs and the
proprietor. Policeman Hickok and Ranahan [*sic*] interfered to keep order,
when remarks were made against Hickok—Wild Bill. In his efforts to
preserve order Samuel Stringham was shot through the head by him and
instantly killed."[33]

Another later version of the fight published in another newspaper in
1876 told a slightly different tale:

*Strawhan and a crowd started to gut a Dutchman's saloon. The rioters
had thrown several glasses on the sidewalk. Bill carried them in with
the remark, "Boys, you hadn't ought to treat a poor man in this way."
Strawhan said he would throw them out again. "Do," retorted Bill,
"and they will carry you out," and they did sure enough, for as Sam
picked up a glass to strike, he fell dead, shot through the neck by the
man who never missed his mark.*[34]

While Hickok wasn't charged in Strawhun's murder, his status as a
lawman was somewhat in dispute after Strawhun's death. Sometime later,
Hickok was attempting to retrieve a prisoner from nearby Fort Hays
named Bob Connors. Connors was being held on a charge of murder and
had been placed in the guardhouse at the fort by Deputy US Marshals
Jack Bridges and C. J. Cox, because it was thought he would not be safe
in the city jail. The post commander, Lt. Colonel George Gibson, had
written to the governor's office for instruction as to who had jurisdiction
over the prisoner. The governor told him to release the prisoner only to
proper legal representatives. Hickok arrived at the post with a warrant for
the arrest of the prisoner from a justice of the peace in Wallace County.

Gibson refused to turn the prisoner over to Wild Bill on the grounds that he did not have a commission as sheriff from the governor and was not the legal authority. The governor responded to Gibson in a letter, "Your refusal to deliver Conners on the demand of Mr. J. B. Hickok meets with my full approval. That person has no legal authority whatever to act as Sheriff of Ellis county, nor under the circumstances through which the vacancy occurred can any Sheriff be chosen until the regular election in November."[35] Apparently, the acting sheriff had been kicked out by the townspeople in favor of installing Hickok as the sheriff, but Hickok did not have a commission from the governor for the job.[36]

Wild Bill's last serious encounter in Hays City was very nearly fatal, but for the misfire of a pistol that had been pressed to his head. The soldiers from nearby Fort Hays, who took their liberty within the city, were notoriously loud and wild and had a tendency to make a lot of trouble. Hickok, as the town lawman, was often called to intervene when they disturbed the peace. But on February 12, 1870, his intervention almost cost him his life. The story goes that two troopers from Fort Hays, Jeremiah Lonergan and John Kile, had left their posts without permission in order to go drink in Hays. They chose to enter Tommy Drum's saloon, which also happened to be the place where Sheriff Wild Bill was spending time. The press reports of exactly what happened to whom and when are predictably confused, and some were published decades after the event. One account, published in 1909, stated the following:

> *Lonergan was a powerful man, and although he had been in the company only a short time he was considered one of the best pugilists of M Troop. When they arrived at the saloon Wild Bill . . . was standing at the bar having a sociable chat with the bar tender. Lonergan walked up behind Wild Bill without being discovered, and as quick as a flash he threw both arms around Wild Bill's neck, from the rear, and pulled him backwards on to the floor, and held his arms out at full length. Lonergan and Wild Bill had had some words before that caused this action. In the meantime Wild Bill got his right hand free and slipped one of his pistols out of his holster. Some of the men visiting this city were in the habit of carrying their pistols stuck down*

in the waistband of their pants, with the hilt protruding, but covered up by their blouse, and a man could whip out one of those pistols in an instant. Kelly [Kile] had his in this position and he immediately whipped it out and put the muzzle into Wild Bill's ear and snapped it. The pistol missed fire, or it would have ended his career then and there. Lonergan was holding Wild Bill's right wrist, but Bill turned his hand far enough to one side to enable him to fire his pistol, and the first shot went through the wrist of Kelly. He fired a second time and the bullet entered Kelly's side, went through his body and could be felt on the other side. Of course Kelly was knocked out of service in a few seconds. Wild Bill did his best to kill Lonergan, who was holding him down, but Lonergan held his wrist in such a position that it was impossible for him to get a shot at his body. He finally fired again and shot Lonergan through the knee cap. That caused Lonergan to release his hold on Wild Bill, who jumped up from the floor and made tracks for the back of the saloon, jumped through a window, taking the glass and sash with him and made his escape. I was on the scene a few moments after Kelly breathed his last. [This is incorrect. Kelly/ Kyle died later at the post-medical facility.] A doctor was sent for. He asked me if Kelly was a friend of mine. I said that he was, and that both men were members of my company. He examined him thoroughly, and then removed a gold ring from Kelly's finger and handed it to me. I kept that ring for a few years, but I never could find any of Kelly's relations, though I tried diligently to do so. I was informed later that his name was Kyle and that he belonged either in Chicago, Illinois or Cincinnati, Ohio. Finally I gave this ring to a friend of mine, John Murphy, who was a trumpeter in my company and was wounded in the battle of the Wichita. The news of this affair very quickly reached camp and a number of the men seized their guns and started for Hayes [sic] City, where I joined the party and we visited all the saloons and dives in the place, but we could not find Wild Bill. If we had found him we will leave it to the reader to imagine what would have happened to him. In the meantime, Kelly's body was taken to our camp and Lonergan was sent to the post hospital at Fort Hayes. I saw Wild Bill about a year later, about 30 miles from Fort Harker on the line of the Kansas-Pacific railroad, either at the little town of Aberdeen or Salina, Kansas, I have forgotten which, while going south in May 1871. Some of the officers and myself and a number of the men had a talk with him. He told us that after leaving Drum's saloon he went to the room that he occupied and took his Winchester rifle and 100 rounds of ammunition and proceeded to a cemetery a little west of town. There he laid until daylight the next morning, as he expected the soldiers would round him up and end his career. He declared that he never intended to be taken alive in that cemetery, and would make many of those soldiers bite the dust before he would be taken. After daylight he left there and started for Big Creek station on the line of the Kansas-Pacific railroad, about eight miles east of the city and boarded a train . . . Wild Bill told me once that he never ran up against a man that he was afraid of in a square pistol duel, but that he did expect sometime some desperado would come up and shoot him from the rear.[37]

# CHAPTER 7

# In Old Abilene

MOST OF THE WESTERN BOOMTOWNS COULD TRACE THEIR EXISTENCE to some advance of civilization over the frontier (such as a railroad or a stage line), or some unique event that drew populace into the city (such as Tombstone and the silver strikes). The city of Abilene was the former—it began as a stage station for the ubiquitous Overland stage lines and gradually gained prominence as the railroad established a terminal there. This still would not have been enough without the cattle industry. Eventually, millions of head of cattle shipped out from dusty Abilene to Chicago or New York, bound for meatpacking plants and the hungry consumers in the East Coast's large urban centers. Abilene was far from this frontier hub when the famed cattleman Joseph McCoy arrived there in 1867. He described it as, ". . . a very small dead place consisting of about one dozen log huts, low small rude affairs, four-fifths of which were covered with dirt for roofing; indeed but one shingle roof could be seen in the whole city. The business of the burg was conducted in two small rooms, mere log huts, and of course the inevitable saloon, also a log hut, was to be found."[1]

Until the coming of the railroad, life in Abilene was rather bleak. The main excitement occurred when a stage rolled into town. The town itself was dirty, windblown, and rather forlorn. The stores were crowded and dirty, and there were no streets to speak of—prairie grass grew wild between buildings and cabins. The most interesting thing about the town was its name, derived from a Biblical reference to a "Tetrach of the Plains" called Abilene.[2]

Wild Bill, circa 1873. SOUTH DAKOTA STATE HISTORICAL SOCIETY

The signs of change were in the air, however, when the Kansas-Pacific Railroad expanded into the small city in 1867. This was the impetus that led cattleman Joe McCoy to invest in the city. He purchased property in the city and began his planning for the expansion of the cattle-buying and shipping business.[3] Once the cattlemen and cowboys began to arrive in large numbers, the face of this sleepy community changed literally overnight.

New businesses and saloons sprang up across the town. There was also a "Drover's Cottage," a hotel of sorts for the cowboys who trailed the herds into town in the summer. It boasted over one hundred rooms and featured such innovations as a laundry and an on-site dining room. It was also known to serve iced drinks—a welcome relief from the humid heat of a Kansas summer.[4] The scale of the investments in Abilene's infrastructure can further be seen in the elaborate saloons and businesses that catered to the cowboy crowd. The most well-known of these—and the fanciest—was the Alamo. The Alamo saloon had two entrances on both ends of the building, one of which had three glass double doors. It had a gorgeous interior with brass fixtures and rails and a large mirror in the back. It had many gaming tables as well as an orchestra, which played several times a day and night.[5]

The customer base for these businesses came chiefly from the drovers, or cowboys, and Texan cattleman, who could be grouped into different classes, mainly distinguishable through economics. The most colorful (and wealthiest) of these were the old-time Southerners who might have been plantation owners before the Civil War. They spent freely and widely and generally were known as gentleman of the old school, but still not against a free-wheeling time while in Abilene. The next group was made up of the less-affluent cattlemen, those who perhaps owned a small ranch. These were the "straight shooters" among the cowmen and were generally family men. They were a part of the lawless doings in town and mainly wanted to conclude their business and exit town in a peaceful and expeditious manner. The dangerous men made up the third group. These drovers were the "hired hands" of the cattle business, the simple trail-driving cowboys. As a rule they did not own a stake in their employers' businesses. They were wage earners and eager to spend those wages in the dives and saloons available in Abilene. This group was also usually armed and frequently intoxicated, a dangerous and often lethal combination. One pioneer remembered that the Texans were frequently armed with Colt 1851 Navy pistols, and if they became intoxicated, they would often use them, no matter the target.[6]

Prostitution was also, of course, a popular business. The city government had some difficulties in this regard, as one particularly noteworthy brothel located itself directly across the street from a school. Eventually the flesh business relocated itself in the north of the town and still later was again moved to a new area of town known as "Fisher's addition." This was all done with the idea of letting the drovers have their "whoop-ups" (which, after all, was the main economic growth industry in this formerly dead little place on the prairie), but without causing the lawlessness that had resulted in the past and its nearness to residents and other businesses.[7]

In the beginning, little effort was made to deal with the lawless elements in Abilene. Most times, affairs were settled privately between parties with a shooting match where the winner was the one who was still alive at the end. This began to change when more progressive-minded citizens realized that there would be no law and order established unless the city was established along formal lines. A group of forty-three citizens presented a petition before a probate judge of Dickinson County, Kansas, requesting the formal incorporation of Abilene into a municipality. This resulted in incorporation and recognition as such by Kansas legal authorities. The first officials in Abilene were appointed by the probate judge as trustees until a regular city election could be held. Initially, the efforts of the new town officials focused on licensing saloons, closing brothels within city limits, and making general attempts to establish some semblance of law and order in the hitherto wild frontier community. A new office of city marshal was created in 1869 as well, and at the same time a city ordinance was also passed that forbade the carrying of firearms within city limits. The thinking was that if the drinking cowboys did not have their guns, they could still get into trouble, but it would be much less serious if it was done without bullets. Construction was also begun on a city jail to hold the offenders. Its first experience with lawbreakers was not reassuring. A black camp cook from one of the cow camps was arrested and held at the jail until a group of cowboys from his camp heard of it, rode into town, forced the release of the prisoner, and shot up the town, even going so far as to force local businesses to close in retaliation for their cook's troubles. This began a series of incidents with cowboy groups ignoring and, in some cases, expressing open defiance against these new city laws.[8]

After initially rejecting his application for city marshal, city officials decided to reconsider the offer of Tom Smith, a man who wanted to be Abilene's first duly appointed city law enforcement officer. Smith was hired in 1869, paid $150 per month, and, as an incentive toward robust police work, was also given $2 for each person convicted whom he had arrested. Smith's first encounters were with cowboys who did not recognize the new anti-firearm ordinance. One particularly notorious lawbreaker in town during 1869 was known as "Big Hank," a cowboy who disobeyed the firearm law and who Smith belted with his fists and disarmed forcibly before driving him out of town. The next day Hank's comrade, "Wyoming Frank," rode into town and tried to confront Smith with a gunfight, whereby Smith applied the same treatment, beat Frank over the head with his own guns, and kicked him out of town. After these very public victories against cowboy lawbreakers, many in Abilene began compliance with the law. Smith was seen by the town fathers as a great success and was even voted a raise to $225 monthly.

Smith's successes also resulted in the establishment of a police court to deal with malefactors of the firearms ordinance. It will never be known if Smith would have been capable of enforcing the law in Abilene effectively when the large groups of drovers began to come in the next summer, as he was murdered by an irate homesteader when he tried to arrest him. This led to a vacancy in the marshal's office that would not be filled until the first general city election in April 1871. The election led to a new mayor, J. G. McCoy, and a new batch of city councilors. Their first order of business was to cement the gains made by Smith in curtailing vice and lawlessness in Abilene. Smith had been effective, but he had not been tested to the degree that was expected to occur when new large Texas herds were driven into town in the next year. They would include large bands of rowdy, armed, and sometimes inebriated cowboys eager to experience a "blow-out" in the saloons and streets of Abilene—what was needed was a strong hand.[9]

Newly elected Mayor McCoy suggested the employment of the newly arrived J. B. "Wild Bill" Hickok as the new town marshal, and his suggestion was adopted unanimously by the city council. Hickok would be paid $150 per month to start plus 25 percent of all the money that came to the city coffers as a result of fines from those Hickok arrested. Hickok's earlier tenure in Hays City had not gone unnoticed, and the famous 1867 article in *Harper's New Monthly Magazine* attributing god-like powers to him was well-known. Hickok's six-foot height, long hair, and piercing blue-gray eyes made him an unusual figure in a time when the average height of an American male was about five feet six inches. Hickok was also known as a careful dresser—someone who strove to make a lasting impression. Curiously, however, for one made famous for his ability with violence and law enforcement, he had a quiet manner and was not known for bluster or "loose talk."

While Smith had enforced the law with his fists, when it was called for, Hickok relied on his guns and fearsome reputation. He was known to resort almost immediately to gun play if the peace and quiet of the city was threatened.[10] He was known as someone who had no fear of a shooting affray. Anyone can get a gun and shoot someone with it. It takes a cat of a different stripe altogether to draw, aim, and fire accurately at a foe when the foe is attempting the same trick upon you. When it came to marksmanship under deadly fire, no one in the West was as effective and deadly as Wild Bill. This was his calling card, his stock and trade, and, as a paid law enforcement officer, his meal ticket.

As the summer of 1871 drew on, Hickok and his particular method of law enforcement became well-known in Abilene. However, the number of Texan cowboys increased throughout the spring and summer, and the town decided that it was simply too much for one lawman, even if that lawman was Wild Bill. The city approved the hiring of several deputies to assist Hickok in his duties. These included Mike Williams, Thomas Carson, "Brocky Jack" Norton, James Gainsford, and James McDonald.[11] Some townspeople criticized Hickok and accused him of allowing his deputies to do too much of his job while he himself supposedly spent too much time at the beautiful Alamo saloon and gambling hall,[12] but it is easy to see that the workload necessitated additional help, even if it was simply for backup for Wild Bill.

One of the more hilarious episodes Hickok took part in was ensuring a quorum was present for a city council meeting. There had been tension on the council over the amount of a new licensing tax on saloons. One faction of the council favored a yearly fee of one hundred dollars, while others thought the fee should be higher. At a meeting where the issue was debated, two hundred dollars was decided as the new licensing fee, but supporters of a lower fee abruptly resigned from the council in protest, leaving the meeting without enough members present for a quorum. The chair instructed Wild Bill to locate one of the missing councilmen, which he did, physically carrying him over his shoulder and bringing him back to the meeting so that new members could be voted on and approved.[13] The local newspaper described the incident and blamed the city mayor, and not Wild Bill, for the actions taken: "A short time since our Mayor, J. G. McCoy, ordered the Marshal to arrest and bring into the meeting of the council, only two members being present, one of the members who did not want to be present. The councilman was arrested and carried into the room by the Marshal. There was not the least shadow of law for such a proceeding, there being no ordinance to compel the attendance of councilmen. Of course the Marshal simply obeyed orders—whether legal or not—and is not to blame."[14]

Hickok generally kept the peace and enforced the city ordinances against the bearing of firearms in city limits, but despite his efforts there were still some shootings and killings that occurred prompting the local newspaper to comment: "If a man is doing any good in the world, his life is worth preserving—but if he is of no use to himself or anybody else, then it don't make much difference how soon his body is put under the ground. And yet, life is sweet to all—and ought to be held sacred by people who are not completely buried in moral darkness."[15]

Despite the lamentations of the newspaper editorialist, life was not held very sacred by a good number of rowdies within Abilene. The town council had been less than willing to enforce city ordinances against prostitution,[16] and perhaps that lack of spine led to the deadly shooting between Hickok and a group of Texans in October 1871—maybe the cowboys felt emboldened by the lack of legal will against their activities.

In any case, the result was predictable—and deadly—and became a touchstone in Wild Bill's career:

*On last Thursday evening a number of men got on a "spree" and compelled several citizens and others to "stand treat" catching them on the street and carrying them upon their shoulders into the saloons. The crowd served the Marshal, commonly called "Wild Bill" in this manner. He treated, but told them that they must keep within the bounds of order or he would stop them. They kept on, until finally one of the crowd, a man named Phil Coe, fired a revolver. The Marshal heard the report and knew at once the leading spirits in the crowd, numbering probably fifty men, intended to put up a fight. He immediately started to quell the affair and when he reached the Alamo saloon, in front of which a crowd had gathered, he was confronted by Coe, who said that he had fired the shot at a dog. Coe had his revolver in his hand, as had also other parties in the crowd. As quick as thought the Marshal drew two revolvers and both men fired almost simultaneously. Several shots were fired, during which Mike Williams, a policeman, came around the corner for the purpose of assisting the Marshal, and rushing between him and Coe received two of the shots intended for Coe. The whole affair was the work of an instant. The Marshal, surrounded by the crowd, and standing in the light, did not recognize Williams, whose death he deeply regrets. Coe was shot through the stomach, the ball coming out through his back; he lived in great agony until Sunday evening; he was a gambler, but a man of natural good impulses in his better moments. It is said that he had a spite at Wild Bill and had threatened to kill him—which Bill believed he would do if he gave him the opportunity. One of Coe's shots went through Bill's coat and another passed between his legs, striking the floor behind him. The fact is that Wild Bill's escape was truly marvelous. The two men were not over eight feet apart, and both of them large, stout men. One or two others in the crowd were hit, but none seriously. We had hoped that the season would pass without any row. The Marshal has, with his assistants, maintained quietness and good order—and this in the face of the fact that at one time during the season there was a larger number of cutthroats and desperadoes in Abilene than in any other town of its size on the continent. Most of them were from Kansas City, St. Louis, New Orleans, Chicago and from the Mountains. We hope no further disturbance will take place. There is no use in trying to override Wild Bill, the Marshal. His arrangements for policing the city are complete and attempts to kill police officers or in any way create disturbance, must result in loss of life on the part of the violators of the law. We hope that all, strangers as well as citizens, will aid by word and deed in maintaining peace and quietness.*[17]

Another paper, the *Junction City Union*, also covered the fight as follows:

*Two men were shot at Abilene Thursday evening. The circumstances were about as follows, so our informant says: Early in the evening a party of men began a spree, going from one bar to another, forcing their acquaintances to treat, and making things howl generally. About 8'o clock, shots were heard in the "Alamo" a gambling hell; whereupon the City Marshal, Haycock [sic] better known as "Wild Bill" made his appearance. It is said that the leader of the party had threatened to kill Bill, "Before frost." As a reply to the Marshal's demand that order should be preserved, some of the party fired upon him, when, drawing his pistols "he fired with marvelous rapidity and characteristic accuracy," as our informant expressed it, shooting a Texan, named Coe, the keeper of the saloon, we believe, through the abdomen, and grazing one or two more. In the midst of the firing, a policeman rushed in to assist Bill but unfortunately got in the line of his fire. It being dark, Bill did not recognize him and supposed him to be one of the party. He was instantly killed. Bill greatly regrets the shooting of his friend. Coe will die. The verdict of the citizens seemed to be unanimously in support of the Marshal, who bravely did his duty.*[18]

By the time of the Coe shooting, Abilene's citizens had become frank admirers of Wild Bill's law enforcement style, especially when large numbers of lawless elements occupied the town and Hickok was all that stood between the scum and the townspeople. Once again, Wild Bill had survived a close quarters' gun battle without a scratch.

From time to time there are those who question "How good was Hickok?" or "Was he really as good as the glamorizers have made out?" Consider this—Hickok was involved in numerous close-quarter shootings in Springfield, Hays City, and Abilene, and not only did he survive each encounter, but his enemies did not. This surely must be the truest test of a gunman's effectiveness, and no one has ever rivaled Wild Bill.

Hickok's remaining days in Abilene were largely uneventful except for a couple of incidents, including a visit by the James and Younger gang in Abilene during Hickok's tenure there, but since they had caused no disturbance, Wild Bill let them alone.[19] Hickok also encountered the bad man John Wesley Hardin in June 1871 when Hardin drifted into Abilene. Hickok apparently became acquainted with Hardin in a friendly way, but once again this was premised on the younger man avoiding disturbances of the peace, which Wild Bill would not allow. Hardin managed to avoid trouble for a time, but then committed his most famous and heinous crime when he shot a fellow boarder at his hotel through the wall for snoring too loudly. Hardin hastened to leave the scene just as Wild Bill and four deputies arrived.[20] It is, of course, difficult to say who would have prevailed if the two of them had been forced to draw on one another, but despite Hardin's fearsome reputation, many of his victims had been ambushed or, as this gentleman was, shot while defenseless—sleeping. Hickok had made his name in face-to-face gunplay, where the other fellow had as much chance to kill as to die. Hickok never shot anyone from ambush or who was not trying to kill him.

Despite Wild Bill's fame and reputation with his pistols (or perhaps partly because of it), he had one more close encounter while engaged in Abilene. Once again, the story was carried in the Abilene *Chronicle*:

*Previous to the inauguration of the present municipal authorities of Abilene, every principle of right and justice was at a discount. No* man's life or property was safe from the murderous intent and lawless invasions of Texans. The state of affairs was very similar to that of Newton during the last season. The law-abiding citizens decided upon a change, and it was thought best to fight the devil with his own weapons. Accordingly Marshal Hickok, popularly known as "Wild Bill" was elected Marshal. He appointed his men, tried and true, as his assistants. Without tracing the history of the great cattle market, it will suffice to say that during the past season there has been order in Abilene. The Texans have kept remarkably quiet, and, as we learn from several citizens of the place, simply for fear of Marshal Hickok and his posse. The Texans, however, viewed him with a jealous eye. Several attempts have been made to kill him, but all in vain. He has from time to time during the last summer received letters from Austin, Texas, warning him of a combination of rangers who had sworn to kill him. Lately, a letter came saying that a purse of $11,000 had been made up and five men were on their way to Abilene to take his life. They arrived in Abilene, but for five days they kept hid, and the marshal, although knowing their presence, was unable to find them. At last, wearied with watching and sleepless nights, and having some business in Topeka, he concluded to come here and take a rest. As he stood on the platform of the depot at Abilene, he noticed four desperate looking fellows headed by a desperado about six foot four inches high. They made no special demonstrations, but when the marshal was about to get on the train, a friend who was with him overheard the big Texan say "Wild Bill is going on the train." He was informed of this remark and kept a watch upon the party. They got on the same train and took seats immediately behind the marshal. In a short time, he got up and took his seat behind them. One of the party glanced around and saw the situation, whereupon they left the car and went into the forward car. The marshal and his friend, then, to be sure that they were after him, went to the rear end of the rear car. The marshal being very tired, sought rest in sleep, while his friend kept watch. Soon the Texans came into the car, and while four of them stood in the aisle, the leader took a position behind the marshal, and a lady who was sitting near, and knew the marshal, saw the Texan grasping a *revolver between his overcoat and dress coat. The marshal's friend, who had been a close observer of the party, went to him and told him not to go to sleep. This occurred about ten miles west of Topeka. When the train arrived in Topeka, the marshal saw his friend safely on the bus and re-entered the car. The party of Texans was just coming out of the door, when the marshal asked them where they were going. They replied, "We propose to stop in Topeka." The marshal then said, "I am satisfied that you are hounding me, and as I intend to stop in Topeka, you can't stop here." They began to object to his restrictions, but a pair of 'em convinced the murderous Texans that they had better go on, which they did. While we cannot justify lawlessness or recklessness of any kind, yet we think the marshal wholly justifiable in his conduct toward such a party.*

*Furthermore, we think he is entitled to the thanks of the law-abiding citizens throughout the state for the safety of life and property at Abilene, which has been secured, more through his daring, than any other agency.*[21]

Wild Bill's official duties in Abilene ended in December 1871— interestingly, the demise of the cattle trade in Abilene swiftly followed. Despite Wild Bill's taming of the rowdier elements in Abilene, the general feeling against the trade was picking up among ordinary citizens. More and more farmers were coming into the city and making it their home, and they brought the old fears about the Texas fever that could be spread to domesticated cattle. These men were influential in the move to ban the Texas cattle trade in Abilene. Feelings waxed for and against, with partisans boosting their positions in editorials in the local newspapers. One writer complained of the high cost of law enforcement to keep order, while another (purportedly the mayor himself) defended the trade in another article and argued that Abilene would have never have been anything without the growth of the trade: "We are informed that when Abilene was first selected as a point to locate this trade, it was an obscure, dingy place, boasting of but one shingle-roofed building, the balance a half-dozen log huts, covered with dirt roofs. As a business place it boasted one little 'whiskey battery,' one eight-by-ten dry goods and grocery house, containing nearly three wheelbarrow loads of goods."[22]

By the winter of 1872, there was enough widespread support against the continuation of the cattle trade in Abilene that a petition was circulated among the populace, and 80 percent of the town's residents signed it. It stated that, "We, the undersigned, members of the Farmer's Protective Association, and officers and citizens of Dickinson county, Kansas, most respectfully request all who have contemplated driving Texas cattle to Abilene the coming season to seek some other point for shipment, as the inhabitants of Dickinson will no longer submit to the evils of the trade."[23] Thus ended Abilene's short burst of fame as a center of cattle shipment—and so also ended Wild Bill's adventures there.

One other item of interest concerning Hickok should be mentioned in regard to Abilene, however. It was there that Hickok met the woman who would become his wife, Agnes Mersman (Lake), an experienced show business woman. She had worked as a horsewoman and high-wire performer, and she had made other various attempts at stage fame since meeting her first husband and the star clown of the Robinson and Eldred Circus near her childhood home in Cincinnati when she was sixteen.[24] The clown's name was Bill Lake, and young Agnes decided to elope with him, and the two were married in Louisiana. The pair worked in various performing troupes and circuses, including the Rich Circus, Spaulding and Rogers Floating Palace, and finally Bill Lake's old employer, the Robinson and Eldred Circus. Eventually the couple formed their own show and were even able to tour Europe, performing for various potentates, including the German emperor. After successful overseas touring, they returned with their show to the United States and began to tour again, until Bill Lake was murdered in Missouri by an irate man who tried to crash the door without buying a ticket. After her first husband's death, Agnes continued to manage the show with some success, and it was in this capacity that she met Wild Bill when her show appeared at Abilene in 1871.[25] There are various accounts of what happened next. One writer claimed that Wild Bill fell instantly and totally in love with Agnes, to the extent that he proposed marriage to her at once, but was politely refused and told to look her up again in a couple of years.[26] The more accepted version is just the opposite—she fell wildly head over heels for Wild Bill, while Hickok maintained a cool composure and refrained from making any solid commitment to her in Abilene. Charles Gross, one of Wild Bill's friends, claimed that Agnes "fell for him hard, fell all the way clear to the basement, tried her best to get him to marry her and run the circus. Bill told me all about it. I said why don't you do it? He said I know she has a good show but when she is done in the West, she will go east and I don't want any paper collar on and it's me for the West, I would be lost back in the states."[27]

The couple did not again have contact until three years later, when Hickok was in New York at the same time Agnes was there.

# CHAPTER 8

# Glory Days

THE NEXT PHASE OF HICKOK'S LIFE, STARTING IN SEPTEMBER 1873, WAS, in some ways, the strangest, as he soon began a career not unlike that of his future wife. Wild Bill's friend, Buffalo Bill Cody, had been making a name for himself around the same time as Hickok. Not unlike Hickok, Cody had a varied career in the West. Cody worked as a scout for the army in Kansas and Nebraska during and after the Civil War, as a buffalo hunter for the railroads in the 1870s, and as a rider for the late, great Pony Express during its short existence. He was also a shrewd businessman and realized that the audiences in large Eastern cities who had devoured the dime novel and pulp magazine stories of Western "heroes" would undoubtedly pay good money to see some of those same individuals on the stage.

In fact Cody's first appearance on the stage was at the instigation of the popular dime novelist Ned Buntline. Cody was already well-known, thanks partly to the lurid tales writers like Buntline had concocted out of his very real accomplishments. However, Cody was a miserable actor in the beginning, forgetting lines and showing great amounts of stage fright, at one point having to be nudged into speaking by Buntline himself. This passed, however, and he grew comfortable with the medium. The show toured for a while, but eventually broke up, as Cody and another performer, Texas Jack, had growing disagreements with Buntline over the split of the show's profits.[1] The Buntline production had been financially successful for 1872 as well as the 1873–1874 performing seasons.

Buffalo Bill, 1895. SOUTH DAKOTA STATE HISTORICAL SOCIETY

Cody set off on his own, and in the beginning, he had presented his tales on the theatrical stage to rave reviews: "The success of Buffalo Bill's theatrical enterprises has been surprisingly great; I say surprisingly because he has scarcely an equal in the mimic arena, being now reckoned the third richest actor in America, notwithstanding that his personal expenses are perhaps greater than those of any character on the stage."[2] Later Cody moved his spectacle into an outdoor format that was hugely successful. His efforts led the great P. T. Barnum to praise Buffalo Bill's showmanship by declaring, "Buffalo Bill the greatest organizer of successful combinations to please public taste in the world."

Cody's later outdoor extravaganzas, which were fully realized three-dimensional exhibitions in wide-open arenas, made his name. One of Cody's biographers described the show:

*The enterprise of which I speak is a vivid illustration of what he calls "Wild Life In The Far West." In it he has associated with himself Dr. W. F. Carver, the acknowledged champion rifle, pistol and shot-gun expert of the world. Cody and Carver are the proprietors of the combination; they have traveling with them during the summer season sixty Indians, as many horses, also herds of elk, buffalo, and the most skillful lariat throwers to be found either in the West or Mexico. Their entertainments are in the open air, being usually given in fair grounds, and consist in shooting, reckless riding, lassoing elk and buffalo, illustrating Indian attacks on stage coaches, in canons, and on settlements. In short, giving a realistic panorama of the wild life through which Buffalo Bill has passed. This brilliant conception is thus far his crowning achievement, and to speak of it as a success does not express the real triumph it has obtained wherever the show has been given. It is a fitting conclusion to the life-long labors of the only Buffalo Bill that the West is capable of bringing into world-wide notice for genuine achievements.*[3]

Cody's efforts were rewarded with monetary success, and he worked to enlist many of his Western acquaintances in his productions.

And Cody approached Wild Bill about appearing in a new show in 1873 called "Scouts of the Plains" featuring himself, Cody, and Texas Jack, essentially portraying themselves before East Cost audiences. Hickok would tour with the company for a short time. However, unlike Cody, Hickok never caught the acting and performance bug. He believed, and said so, that the three of them were making public fools of the themselves, as Buffalo Bill wrote concerning Hickok: "Although he had a fine stage appearance, was a handsome fellow and possessed a good, strong voice, yet when he went upon the stage before an audience, it was almost impossible for him to utter a word. He insisted that we were making a set of fools of ourselves, and that we were the laughing stock of the people."[4]

According to Cody, Hickok was a fun-loving performer, in spite of his misgivings about the reputation they were making for themselves. Cody would later say, "Wild Bill was continually playing tricks on the members of the company, and it was his especial delight to torment the 'supers.' Quite frequently, in our sham Indian battles, he would run up to the Indians (supers) and putting his pistol close to their legs fire and burn them with the powder instead of shooting over their heads. This would make them dance and jump, so that it was difficult to make them fall and die—although they were paid twenty-five cents each for performing the 'dying business.'"[5]

The initial performances of "Scouts of the Plains" were enormously popular with audiences and filled with comedy and action. At one point Hickok was supposed to take a swig of "whiskey" from a bottle, but after doing so, he spit out the liquid when he found out it was cold tea. The audience loved it.[6] Even there, in the world of the stage and play, Hickok's reputation continued to draw challengers who would have challenged him and lived to brag about it. Cody told a story of one night when Wild Bill's reputation preceded him:

*One day at Titusville, Pennsylvania, while Burke, the business agent was registering our names and making arrangements for our accommodation, several of us started for the billiard room, but were met by the landlord, who stopped me [Cody] and said that there was a party of roughs from the lower oil regions who were "spreeing," and*

Three famous Westerners: Wild Bill, Texas Jack, and Buffalo Bill, circa 1873–1874.

*had boasted that they were in town to meet the Buffalo Bill gang and clean them out. The landlord begged of me not to allow the members of the troupe to enter the billiard room as he did not wish any fight in his house. To please the landlord, and at his suggestion, I called the boys up into the parlor and explained to them the situation. Wild Bill wanted to go at once and fight the whole mob, but I persuaded him to keep away from them during the day . . . In order to entirely avoid the roughs the members of the company entered the theatre through a private door from the hotel, as the two buildings joined each other. While I was standing at the door of the theatre taking tickets, the landlord came rushing up and said that Wild Bill was having a fight with the roughs in the bar-room. It seemed that Bill had not been able to resist the temptation of going to see what kind of mob it was that wanted to test the pluck of the Buffalo Bill party; and just as he stepped into the room, one of the bruisers put his hand on Bill's shoulder and said: "Hello Buffalo Bill! We have been looking for you all day." "My name is not Buffalo Bill; you are mistaken in the name," was the reply.*

Texas Jack, Wild Bill, Buffalo Bill, circa 1873. SOUTH DAKOTA STATE HISTORICAL SOCIETY

*"You're a liar!" said the bruiser. Bill instantly knocked him down and then seizing a chair he laid out four or five of the crowd on the floor, and then drove the rest out of the room. All this was done in a minute or two, and by the time I got down stairs, Bill was coming out of the bar-room, whistling a lively tune. "Well!" said he, "I have been interviewing that party that wanted to clean us out." "I thought you promised to come into the Opera House by the private entrance?" "I did try to follow that trail, but I got lost among the canons and then I ran in among the hostiles," said he; "but it's alright now; they won't bother us anymore."*[7]

By all accounts, despite his professed love for the West and its environs and in spite of his misgivings about their portrayal, Hickok enjoyed his time touring with Cody and took advantage of the big city nightlife when possible, especially when it came to his favorite diversion, poker. When the show was in Portland, Maine, Hickok had retired to the hotel where they were staying for the evening when he was disturbed by increasing noises from the room next door. But, "finding at length that the noise increased with no likelihood of abating soon, he got up with the intention of either suppressing the racket or having a first-class row. In partial undress he knocked at the door of his unknown neighbors only to find that the room was occupied by five of Portland's leading businessmen and that their noise was the result of a game of poker, spiced with liquid refreshments of savory perfume. Before making known the purpose of his visit, the party invited him to join them in the game and partake of the bottle that was nigh well empty. Nothing ever afforded Bill so much pleasure as a game of poker, and to indulge this gratification he was always ready to sacrifice a night's rest. He therefore entered into the sport of the game and after playing until the party were fairly exhausted both in body and purse, he got up from the table seven hundred dollars better off than when he sat down. In order that such pleasant company might not separate without some benefit, he generously gave them this parting advice, 'Gentlemen, I appreciate your hospitality and especially the good luck in which I have played tonight, therefore I will tell you a little secret, for it may prove very valuable to you all hereafter; never wake up a stranger, destroy his rest and invite him to take a hand in a game of poker with you. Good night.'"[8]

Hickok also had various shocks as he adapted to life touring through the great cities. Once, according to Cody, Hickok forcibly objected to the five-dollar charge for a carriage ride in New York:

*When I had arranged terms with Wild Bill to appear with my company, we were in New York playing an engagement, and I was stopping at the Metropolitan Hotel. Bill arrived in New York after dark, and being unacquainted with the city—this being his first visit there—he took a hack, instructing the driver to take him to the Metropolitan Hotel. Upon arriving at the house, Bill asked the driver his charges. "Five dollars sir," was the reply. "And you wouldn't accept anything less would you?" asked Bill. "No sir, that's the charge and nothing less." Bill then handed the driver five dollars at the same time striking him a blow in the face that sent him plowing up the settlings of the gutter. A policeman very soon came after Bill, but bail being furnished by me, he was kept out of the tombs; but the next day I paid a fine of $10 for him. This was his first experience in New York."[9]*

Hickok broke ranks with Cody and left the "Scouts of the Plains" in March 1874 in Rochester, New York. Before he left, Texas Jack and Cody between them gave Hickok one thousand dollars as a parting gift of friendship.[10] And the local Rochester paper reported extensively on Wild Bill's exit from show business:

*Having seen the stalwart form of Wild Bill (J. B. Hickok) passing down State Street yesterday afternoon, and knowing that the troupe of scouts with which he has been appearing upon the stage for some time past had departed for Lockport where they performed last night, we ventured to approach the hero and enquire the reason why he tarried behind his fellows. Our hand was grasped with considerable warmth in his which appeared to be an iron vice from which we were glad to be released. After devoting a few words not at all complimentary to the blustering March winds that were whirling snow through the streets, he began to relate why he was not with the troupe, and we should have had the whole matter explained then and there had not an impudent youngster crying, "Union or Express" come down the street with the loud cry of "Oh stag his ribs with the long hair!" Now it is well known that Bill wears his hair in the flowing style prevalent on the frontier, and this, together with the tall form and manly deportment of the man, attracted the attention of the newsboy and caused him to give vent to several exclamations of no particular importance to the student of polite literature, but very well calculated to draw the attention of everyone within the sound of his voice to us. Bill was not at all affected by this strange proceeding. He remarked that he had witnessed it in hundreds of towns, so often in fact, that it was an old thing to him. We suggested, however, that we should move along, to which he willingly consented. The few staring mouth-opened children of the pave who had gathered were soon left behind, and as we passed into Exchange Place, there was but one left, and he took to his heels because Wild Bill stopped and looked at him. We were then informed that Bill had received a call to the frontier.*

*Recognized as one of the best scouts and Indian fighters that have appeared upon the great Western frontier, his services are highly valued and eagerly sought for when there is danger of war with the Red man. Just now there is considerable commotion at Fort Laramie and some of the Indian agencies, especially the Red Cloud and Spotted Tail agencies. The Sioux has been seen in his war paint and General Sheridan thinks he may begin his attempt to seek the paleface in few weeks. At this time and amid such scenes as these, the services of Wild Bill will be invaluable to the United States troops. It is this, together with a longing desire to return to the free, wild life he loves so well that has called our hero away. He will first proceed to New York where he has some business to transact, remain there a few days and then go direct to the frontier. Buffalo Bill, Texas Jack and the other scouts did not like to have him leave, but when he said he must go, the noble-hearted fellows presented him with $500 apiece, and gave him a splendid revolver, bidding him to make good use of it among the "Reds." He had nothing but kind words to speak of the boys, as* *he familiarly termed the other scouts. He wished them all manner of good fortune and was sure they would receive it. Wild Bill is a noble fellow, a true-hearted child of nature, one of those men which one occasionally comes in contact with and ever after retains a place in his memory. We shook hands with the hero, bade him goodbye, and wished him a pleasant journey to his far western home. He left at 12:15 this morning for New York.*[11]

There may be more to the story than that Hickok simply answered a "call to the frontier." Wild Bill enjoyed playing tricks on members of the show and rumor had it that Cody became exasperated with his antics, including his continuing practice of firing his pistol near the legs of the "supers," as the Indian impersonators were called, and burning their legs with powder burns. Hickok had been warned to stop this practice earlier, but apparently resumed it again. This may have been the last straw for Cody, who confronted Hickok on this point once again, and shortly thereafter Hickok left the show.[12]

It is also possible that one of the reasons Hickok left the show was his renewed acquaintance with Agnes Lake. She was in Rochester and attended the performance. Cody saw her and told Hickok, who met her and discussed their relationship, proposing marriage. Agnes said that her business was in such a state of disarray that she could not possibly consider marriage for at least two years. Hickok reluctantly agreed, and they parted from each other until their eventual marriage in Cheyenne, Wyoming Territory in 1876.[13]

There was some further drama with show business for Hickok even after his departure. Hickok left Rochester for New York City, lost heavily in the games of chance he so dearly loved, and, due to his penury, was persuaded by another theatrical troupe to join a performing show again. He tried this for a few weeks, but the show went bankrupt. Hickok left the show after this, but the show's manager opened the show again and, realizing the enormous drawing power of Wild Bill's presence, hired a look-alike and advertised this knock-off as the real man. This worked for a time, until the real Wild Bill heard of this deception and reportedly attended a performance of the show. As the story goes, Hickok interrupted the show with the usurper by jumping onstage and throwing his impersonator into the orchestra pit. Police were called to arrest him. Hickok reportedly confronted the first officer who approached him by asking if he was alone. When told the officer was by himself, Wild Bill advised him to get reinforcements before he attempted to take him into custody. Reinforcements duly arrived in the form of a sheriff and another policeman. They finally persuaded Hickok to surrender without incident. He was fined three dollars for his bad conduct and released.[14]

There were also unsubstantiated reports that during the last few weeks of his performing career, Hickok's vision had begun to bother him. He may have shot out a spotlight that was shining too brightly on his face during one performance, and it was said that he threatened to shoot out another during a performance in Philadelphia as well.[15] If the rumors were true, this must have been very troubling to Hickok. There could hardly be a worse misfortune to befall a famed gunfighter than trouble with vision. Hickok was famous for the men he had killed, and it was only too likely that many of these men had friends or relatives who would gladly take a chance against him—especially if it became known that he was no longer the formidable man he had been. It is difficult to say just what the malady may have been, but in symptoms it sounds like the beginning of glaucoma or cataracts, unusual in someone so young, but not unheard of, especially considering that Hickok had spent literally thousands of hours in dimly lit saloons inhaling copious amounts of secondhand smoke during his years as a peace officer. The other possibility is that Wild Bill suffered from a condition known in the nineteenth century as "ophthalmia," an eye deficiency brought on sometimes from untreated gonorrhea.[16]

# CHAPTER 9

# Sunset

AFTER HICKOK PARTED COMPANY WITH CODY IN 1874 AND THEN LEFT behind his other theatrical pursuits as well, there came a period of time when it is difficult to verify his exact actions and whereabouts. According to one source, he drifted west to Cheyenne, Wyoming Territory, and walked into a gambling den maintained by a man named Boulder. Bill had two hundred dollars in his pocket and entered into a faro game, betting cautiously. After losing most of his money, however careful he had been, Hickok was informed by Boulder that the limit was twenty-five dollars and he would not play above that sum, "Why, didn't you just take $50 of my money?" said Hickok. "Well, I won't let you play that amount anymore," replied Boulder. "You won't?" said Bill, "then I'll see why; that fifty dollar bill lays on the tray, and if my card don't turn, the money is yours, but if does come out, then I'll have fifty dollars of your money or there'll be fun here, that's all." From this a war of words followed, until Bill struck Boulder on the head with a heavy walking cane, which rolled him off a substantial seat. Several bouncers for the establishment rushed upon Bill, but he knocked them in a most artistic manner, until finding the fighting too progressive, he jumped into a corner and jerked out two pistols. At this juncture the barkeeper attending the saloon downstairs, hearing the noise, ran up, discovered the situation, and cried out, "Look out boys, that's Wild Bill!" This information acted like magic; the tempest was becalmed, and a moment later Bill was alone."[1]

Hickok was also supposedly involved in a shooting in Cheyenne, when the brother of Phil Coe, the cowboy/gambler that he shot and killed in Abilene while serving as a peace officer there, caught up with him at a bar owned by Luke Murrin. Hickok is supposed to have seen Coe and an accomplice come into the bar, because he was looking into a large mirror at the back of the room that showed the entrance behind him. Hickok then fired behind him with the aid of the mirror, killing Coe. He then threw his pistol at Coe's accomplice and threw him on the bar, breaking his neck. Hickok was supposedly arrested for the killings, but he was eventually released, as these were considered justifiable homicides.[2] There is no evidence to verify this story—it is probably another example of Hickok's reputation being so big that biographers felt they could take liberties with the truth and no one would question their stories.

Another Westerner who encountered Hickok after his years in show business was Doc Carver, a Western performer and showman along the lines of Buffalo Bill. Carver had several interactions with Hickok and related one of them in detail. Carver claimed that after a period of hunting and trapping in Nebraska, Hickok supposedly engaged in a gunfight with three men in Sidney, Nebraska, killing all three, but once again documentation of this adventure is lacking.[3]

Hickok was no longer officially employed as a peace officer, and he would probably be best described as a professional gambler. He was supposedly included on a 1876 city list of vagrants who should leave Cheyenne at one point during his time there. In a story that appeared after Hickok's death, the Cheyenne *Daily Leader* ran Hickok into the ground, describing him as all talk and no action—possibly justifying the charge of vagrancy:

> *Wild Bill was one of those characters developed by the onward strides of the iron horse when the Great American Desert was spanned by the Pacific railways. Seven or eight years ago his name was prominent in the "Scare-Heads" of the border press and if we could believe the half of what was written concerning his daring deeds, he must certainly have been one of the bravest and most scrupulous characters of those lawless times. Contact with the man however dispelled all these allusions, and of late years Wild Bill seems to have become a very tame and worthless loafer and bummer. Our city marshal ordered*

*him out of town by virtue of the provision of the vagrant act, only a few months ago, but Bill cordially invited the officer to go to a much warmer clime than this and expressed the intention of staying there as long as he pleased. Bill delighted in joining a crowd of tenderfeet at the bar and soaking himself with whiskey at their expense, while he stuffed them in return with . . . tales of his thrilling adventures . . . Years ago, before wine and women had ruined his constitution and impaired his faculties, he was more worthy of the fame which he attained on the border."[4]*

The claim of vagrancy was denied later by the city peace officer, Marshal Slaughter, who wanted to distance himself from any allegation that he had ordered a man as famous as Wild Bill to leave town. Slaughter made his statement in another of Cheyenne's newspapers, and the Cheyenne *Daily Leader* responded with a taunting article directed against the Marshal. "City Marshal Slaughter rushes into print with the statement that Wild Bill was never ordered to leave town, and by so doing confesses his ignorance of a matter which he should have been cognizant of. It may be true that Slaughter never ordered Bill to leave town, but we can prove that Bill was ordered out of town on several occasions by both city and county officers . . . By the way, was the Marshal afraid of Wild Bill?"

Vagrant or not, Hickok was a well-known figure out and about in Cheyenne. He made himself known to several individuals who have left accounts of his appearance and temperament—seemingly at odds with his reputation as a brash drunkard, as portrayed in some newspaper stories. Annie Tallent, an early settler in the Black Hills, described her memorable encounter with Wild Bill in Cheyenne in 1875:

*One day during the summer of 1875, while walking along one of the principal streets of Cheyenne with a friend, there appeared sauntering leisurely along towards us from the opposite direction, a tall, straight and rather heavily built individual in ordinary citizen's clothes, sans revolvers and knives, sans buckskin leggings and spurs, and sans everything that would betoken the real character of the man, save that he wore a broad-brimmed sombrero hat and a profusion of light*

Black Hills gold prospectors, circa 1889. SOUTH DAKOTA STATE HISTORICAL SOCIETY

*brown hair hanging down over his broad shoulders. A nearer view betrayed the fact that he also wore a carefully cultivated mustache of a still lighter shade, which curled up saucily at each corner of his somewhat sinister mouth, while on his chin grew a small hirsute tuft of the same shade, and barring the two latter appendages he might have easily been taken for a Quaker minister [!]. When within a few feet of us, he hesitated a moment, as if undecided, then stepping to one side suddenly stopped, at the same time doffing his sombrero and addressing me in good respectable Anglo–Saxon vernacular substantially as follows: "Madame, I hope you will pardon my seeming boldness, but knowing that you recently returned from the Black Hills, I take the liberty of asking a few questions in regard to that country, as I expect to go there myself soon. My name is Hickok." I bowed low in acknowledgement of the supposed honor but I must confess that his next announcement somewhat startled me. "I am sometimes called Wild Bill," he continued, "and you have no doubt heard of me, although," he added, "I suppose you have heard nothing good of me." "Yes," I replied candidly, "I have often heard of Wild Bill and his rep-*

*utation, to say the least, is not at all creditable to him. But," I hastened to add, "perhaps he is not so black as he has been painted." "Well, as to that," he replied, "I suppose I am called a red-handed murderer, which I deny. That I have killed men I admit, but never unless in absolute self-defense, or in the performance of an official duty. I never, in all my life, took any mean advantage of an enemy. Yet understand," he added, with a dangerous gleam in his eye, "I never allowed a man to get the drop on me. But perhaps I may yet die with my boots on," he said, his face softening a little. Ah, was this a premonition of the tragic fate that awaited him? After making a few queries relative to the Black Hills, which were politely answered, Wild Bill, with a gracious bow that would have done credit to a Chesterfield, passed on down the street out of sight, and I never heard more of him until one day in August 1876, when the cry of "Wild Bill is shot!" was carried along the main street of Deadwood.[5]*

It was also in March 1876 that Wild Bill managed to wed Agnes. A newspaper story from Cheyenne, Wyoming, announced the event: "Married-by the Rev. W. F. Warren, March 5th, 1876 at the residence of S. L. Moyer, Cheyenne, Wyoming Territory, Mrs. Agnes Lake Thatcher of Cincinnati Ohio to James Butler Hickok, Wild Bill of this city."[6] The new couple had very little time together, however, as Hickok left her two weeks after the wedding to pursue gold in the Black Hills.

# CHAPTER 10

# The Black Hills

.

IN THE SPRING OF 1875, HICKOK AND TWO FRIENDS, TOM BUSEY AND AN
old trapper named Doc McGregor, decided to set out on an expedition
to the Black Hills to follow the rumors of gold in the region. The group
left Cheyenne and headed along Sage Creek to the confluence of the
Cheyenne River, and they followed the main stream to French Creek.
The party decided to travel a bit farther on and constructed a comfortable
cabin. They began explorations for gold in the creeks and remained well
supplied with wild game. They did not see any Indians near their camp
and perhaps lapsed into a false sense of security. According to one story
that lacks documentation or evidence, in April 1875 Wild Bill left the
cabin to retrieve water for their supper and happened to see a gray fox
near the creek. The fox's fur was valuable, and Hickok tried to shoot it but
only wounded the creature, which ran away. Wild Bill followed and was
gradually led several miles away in this chase. He failed to retrieve the
fox and headed back toward the cabin, but he heard the sounds of Indian
cries coming from there. He made it back near the cabin and saw that
it had been sacked and burned by approximately twenty Indians, who
he identified as Sioux. His friends were presumed dead, and he would
join them unless he could contrive an escape. Hickok fled all that night
and into the next day on foot when he could see Indians in pursuit on
the horizon. Hickok rapidly lost ground to his mounted pursuers, and
he was forced to jump from a high bank into the nearby Beaver Creek,
where he managed to land in some deep water and emerge unharmed.
Eventually the Indians caught up with him, but he had climbed a tree for

the night and a tremendous rain began to fall. The Indians were trapped in the low-lying creek bed and were washed away by the flood. Hickok managed to make his way to the safety of Fort Fetterman.[1]

The story is probably an embellishment or outright creation of Hickok biographer J. W. Buel, who liked to add a dash of "flavor" to the truth, and who probably took the framework for the event from another incident that occurred in the region. In any case, it does accurately describe the danger any white man faced if he entered the Black Hills in search of gold. It also shows the type of exploits that were popularly attributed to Hickok on a regular basis in the popular media. His reputation was undoubtedly enhanced by stories such as this—true or not. Hickok's authenticated adventures in the Black Hills began after the 1874 Custer expedition discovered gold and started the great rush that led to the creation of the city of Deadwood. While it is generally believed that gold was first discovered in the Black Hills by soldiers under General Custer, there is evidence of earlier gold-seekers in the region. One of the most interesting events in the history of the area involved the discovery of the "Thoen" Stone. The Thoens were two brothers who were residents of Spearfish, South Dakota, and who had purchased some rocky property near the town and were using the stony land to quarry stone for a residence. While thus engaged, they uncovered a stone about twelve inches square that had some distinctive markings inscribed upon it. They took the rock home and washed it off and discovered that there were words on the rock as follows, "Came to these Hills in 1833, seven of us, De Lacompt-Ezra Kind, G.W. Wood-T. Brown-R. Kent- Wm. King- Indian Crow-m all dead but me, Ezra Kind, killed by Indians beyond the high hill, got our gold June 1834." It was inscribed on the other side as follows, "Got all the gold we could carry, our ponies all got by the Indians I have lost my gun and nothing to eat and Indians hunting me."[2] This rather depressing account is nonetheless generally accepted as proof that early prospectors were traipsing the Black Hills as early as the 1830s in search of gold.

Another interesting, but unproven story relates the fate of a small group of fifteen or sixteen gold-seekers who entered the Hills in 1852. Their story, related in the book *The Coming Empire* by Judge Horatio

Maguire, is worth repeating, because it is almost identical to the story that biographer Buel told about Wild Bill and his adventures prospecting and escaping from Indians in the Black Hills. There can be little doubt that Buel plagiarized his account from the following story. Maguire wrote that:

*The forgoing facts seem sufficiently well authenticated. I think there is no reasonable doubt that the signs of old mining operations so numerously found in the Black Hills, are evidences left behind by the unfortunate little party of adventurers who went thither from Fort Laramie in 1852. It is equally certain that they were all, save the three who went through to California, and probably one other, massacred by the Indians. The reader will be given what the author knows of one having escaped of the sixteen who remained in the Hills. Hearing that information could be had at Salt Lake City of a man having escaped from an Indian massacre, somewhere north of the North Platte, in the fall of 1852. I wrote to an old mountain friend at that place to make inquiries in regard to the matter. My correspondent has furnished me with some apparently conclusive facts. He found a man, named Hale, reported to be veracious, and an old settler of Utah, who made a statement that seems to solve the mystery of the fate of fifteen of the sixteen missing prospectors . . . About the 10th of October 1852, a pitiable wreck of a man, with deep sullen, wild-bleering eyes, skin seemingly clinging to the very bones of his skeletal frame, his scanty raiment in tatters, with the legs of a pair of old boots wrought into a sort of sandal-protection for his otherwise exposed feet, came hobbling, just after nightfall into a camp of Mormon hunters on the Green River. He was in the last stage of starvation and could not have lived many hours longer . . . The rough but kind frontiersman, knowing it would be certain death to allow him to eat to satiety, fed him a quantity of strengthening broth, and furnished him with a comfortable bed of robes . . . He gave his name as Thomas Renshaw, formerly of Cincinnati Ohio, Said he was one of a party of prospectors who had turned north from the North Platte emigrant road, at Fort Laramie, to hunt for gold mines which "friendly" Indians had told them existed in the Black Hills. Entering the Hills on the south, with two ox teams and several saddle horses, they sank shafts and found gold; but not in satisfying quantities. They then cached their wagons, packed their oxen and horses with supplies and penetrated the interior, finding a little gold everywhere, and very good prospects on a clear, swift river about four days travel from where they first struck the mountains [undoubtedly Rapid Creek]; but they could not open ground there owing to the great quantity of water flowing into the shafts. They then went on farther north, traveling four days over rough, high ridges, and through some dense forests and network of fallen timber—unable to make over seven or eight miles a day—when they descended from a high mountain into a deep gorge, through which flowed a little stream. [This description applies to Whitewood Creek, near the south of Deadwood.] They got down to bed-rock on this little stream, without difficulty, and found prospects ranging from ten to twenty cents to the pan. At this juncture, three or four weeks having elapsed since they turned off from the emigrant road, three of the party started back, to report the discovery to friends on their way to California . . . The party then hewed out sluicing lumber, and had one string of sluices in operation, yielding from an ounce to an ounce and a half a day to the hand, and were busily engaged getting timbers for more, when Indians came upon them, murdering them all but the narrator. Continuing his narration, Renshaw said he went out one morning to kill a deer, and did not return until late in the afternoon. Approaching the camp, he noticed unusually large volumes of smoke rising from the gulch, which excited his apprehension, and caused him to approach covertly; and these first fears were soon confirmed by his hearing a medley of piercing, wild yells. Throwing aside the meat he was carrying, he crept up to the brink of the mountain over the camp, and, looking down, beheld a blood-curdling scene. The prospector's shack, or brush-covered tents, were ablaze, and around the bonfire a hundred savages were engaged in a fiendish dance, his companions' reeking scalps—fastened to the end of poles, and passed from hand to hand in the demoniacal demonstrations, being the leading features in the horrible orgies. Renshaw waited until nightfall, when he forced his way through the forests, as best he could, in a southwesterly direction, hoping to reach the emigrant road a distance west of Fort Laramie, and intercept a wagon train. He had a few matches, his rifle and a small supply of ammunition, and, as he passed through a country abounding with game, he did not suffer from hunger, to any great extent, the first three or four weeks; but he dared not make a fire to cook with, except in the most secluded places, and suffered extremely from the chilling night air. He also had a pocket compass, and knew the general direction he should take—knew if he could continuously bear to the southwest he would emerge upon the North Platte road, if he lived long enough to reach it; but to follow a general direction, in such a country, was not so easy. He soon found his way blocked with savage cliffs, which could not be scaled, necessitating long and tortuous efforts to pass them by circuitous routes; and he frequently suffered from thirst, when lost and bewildered among the savage crags of the divides. Finally he succeeded in reaching the plateau country between the head of the South Fork of the Cheyenne and the North Fork of the Platte. But his last match was gone, his last bullet fired, and his greatest sufferings were yet to be endured. Hunger began to gnaw, and his tongue was often parched with thirst. The soles of his boots were gone and his clothing had been literally torn from his person by the thorns of the innumerable thickets he had passed through. His strength was rapidly failing and his gun and accoutrements, all save his knife, were cast aside as useless encumbrances. Thenceforth his main dependence for subsistence were chokecherries, which he occasionally found in the ravines, and the pulpy part of the prickly pear leaf, juicy and somewhat nourishing, from which he stripped the outside skin with his knife. This succulent plant, which abounds in those regions, was to him both food and drink; he would have perished of thirst in some of the long stretches between water had it not been for the moisture it afforded. Roots, too, when procured, were eagerly devoured. At last the emigrant road was reached; but the last train, for that year, had passed, and that unfortunate man, his strength nearly exhausted, and suffering intensely from excruciating pains of various kinds, especially internal gripings caused by the unnatural food he was forced to eat, felt that he had only reached it to leave his skeleton there as a mute and ghastly witness of his horrible fate. But as long as there is life there is hope is a sentiment that animates to the last, and he wearily pushed on to the westward, traveling, for the most part, after dark, and sleeping through the warm hours of the day, until he joyfully saw the smoke curling from the camp-fire of his rescuers.*[3]

It was fairly common for one writer to take and make use of someone else's work in the nineteenth century, but more important, the repetition of the events in print casts further doubt on the idea that Wild Bill was ever in the Black Hills prior to his final sojourn in Deadwood, especially in a wild area overrun with Indians.

Custer and his troops had set off from Fort Abraham Lincoln on July 2, 1874, with orders to explore the Black Hills and penetrate to the interior. The large, well-armed party had little to fear from the Sioux, unlike the smaller contingents of individual prospectors who had entered the region earlier. Custer and his force entered the Black Hills near present Sundance, Wyoming, and made their way to the southern area around

Deadwood about 1930. SOUTH DAKOTA STATE HISTORICAL SOCIETY

Harney Peak. There they established a permanent camp of French Creek and began exploring the area. They made it back to the fort on August 30.

It is difficult to ascertain who was the discoverer of the gold on this expedition, but investigations made by a president of the Black Hills School of Mines made in the 1920s stated, "That two practical miners, Horatio Ross and William McKay accompanied the expedition; that on arrival in the vicinity of Custer, on July 27th, they began panning the creek gravels for gold; that one of them, or both together, obtained color on that date, along Castle Creek; and that such discovery may have been at any time between July 27th and August 2nd; and that it may have been on French Creek where permanent camp was made."[4] Another member of the expedition, William Curtis, who was a newspaperman, wrote a letter to his newspaper the Chicago *Inter Ocean*, July 27, 1874, which stated, "Yesterday, July 26th, for the first time were found indications of gold and today we remained in camp while parties have gone out prospecting in every direction." He also noted on August 3, "The discovery was made on the 2nd of August in the bed of a creek we suppose is French Creek on the maps, and the yield was about thirty-five cents in dust to three pans."[5] Horatio Ross is also quoted in *South Dakota and Western Advocate* as stating that he and his partner discovered gold: "On the morning of July 30th 1874, my partner McKay and I took our miner's pans and went down to the bank of French Creek and discovered gold in the gravel of the stream."[6]

One of the problems for prospective gold-seekers, once word leaked out of the discovery of the valuable metal, was the fact that the goldfields were deep in the Black Hills, which was by treaty, the land of the Sioux Indians. Two expeditions, named after its leader John Gordon, tried to avoid US soldiers and enter the goldfields in 1874 and 1875 with mixed results.[7] Soldiers were ordered to turn back any prospective gold-seekers who entered the region, as per the treaty with the Sioux.

Wild Bill would have heard rumors of the gold rush in Wyoming and had certainly heard of the boomtown of Deadwood, where he would have some of his most famous adventures and meet his demise. The probable first prospector and first settler in what is now Deadwood was William Smith. He and his party of four men entered the Hills from the Montana side in August 1875 and traveled through the Black Hills.

They met with no trouble and set up camp in what later became known as "Smith Gulch" near the present town of Deadwood, where they found gold in the stream nearby. The Blanchard party had also entered the Black Hills from the south and discovered gold in what became known as "Deadwood Gulch," so they both get the credit for being "first finders."[8]

Word began to seep out of the gold strikes, principally as the prospectors needed to resupply themselves, and they were forced to send men out for various staples to last their first winter. Eventually there became a trickle, then a flood, of new miners venturing into the Deadwood area, eager to have a try at the placer gold in the area. All certainly realized that their entire operation was a violation of federal policy, as they were on Sioux territory. Many feared that they would be forcibly evicted by troopers of the US Army. Probably what saved the miners from being arrested and vacated from their claims was the speed of migration into the area. In about one year's time, Deadwood went from a small miners' camp with tents and primitive conditions to a fully formed city with hundreds of buildings, stores, saloons, and businesses, all catering to the rough prospectors who hoped to strike it rich in the nearby hills. As was the case with almost every case of Western gold or silver strikes, the real millionaires were often the store owners who capitalized on the sudden wealth of the prospectors by charging outrageous prices for ordinary supplies and luxury goods. Some of these businesses were memorable for various reasons, but all were unique because they were all technically illegal. A dance hall was opened in May 1876 on the corner of Main and Sine Streets. It featured dance girls and a bar and was reportedly very popular. Shortly after, there was the "Gem Theater," which drove the first dance hall out of business. Main Street was crowded with various saloons and gambling halls, attempting to fleece the unwary. There were also numerous con artists present, including the famous "Soapy" Taylor, so named because he sold small packs of soap, some of which contained one or five dollar bills. He would entice customers by showing them the soap with the money then quickly switch the package to one with no money, and thus he made a tidy profit from his "soap shell game."[9]

The first "faro-bank" was also located nearby. Known as the "Wide West Saloon," it featured the first faro bank in Deadwood and catered to the gambling crowd. There was also a Keno game available at the "Eureka Hall," another gambling den located across the street from the faro-bank. A well-known saloon of a "higher class" was known as the "Melodeon." The Melodeon featured music and entertainers and was usually filled nightly. Also nearby was the "Saloon No. 10," and directly across the street from No. 10 was the notorious Gem Theatre. Its promoter, Al Swearengen, was essentially a human trafficker, specializing in persuading young women from outside the Black Hills to come with him to Deadwood, promising them good and legitimate jobs at hotels or eateries. Once the women were in Deadwood and under his power, he virtually imprisoned them in prostitution at the Gem. He constructed a series of small rooms at the rear of the building that were used for the purpose of renting out "his" girls for sexual encounters with miners, gamblers, and anyone else who could pay with ready cash.[10] These prostitutes were well-known in Deadwood, even by children. Estelline Bennett, in her memoir, *Old Deadwood Days*, described the atmosphere and personalities she witnessed in Deadwood as a child there in the 1870s:

> *The lovely light ladies—pretty, beautifully gowned and demure mannered—were, many of them, known by face and name to everybody. But their little span of glory was too brief to leave any illusion in our mind about the desirability of such lives. They collected their wages of sin under our very eyes. We saw them on the street, in the stores, at the theater on the rare occasions when there was a play at Nye's Opera House or Keimer Hall. And then, two or three years later, we saw these same girls pallid and shabby, with dingy old "fascinators" over their heads, slipping furtively down the alley that ran back of Main street, in quest of the price of a drink or a shot of dope. Once in a long time one of them married and escaped this fate.[11] Some of them avoided it by the route of poison or the little gun. Without anyone calling our attention to it, we accepted the drab skulking procession as the inevitable end of the easiest way.[12]*

There was also the human detritus that was the inevitable consequence of the great wealth that came from the goldfields and the gambling of those who lost their money in Deadwood. One example was "Swill Barrel Jimmy," a ruined gambler who wore a long frock coat and derby, hinting at his origins as possibly a former man of substance, perhaps even a Southern gentleman or Confederate officer. He was reduced to begging his meals from the backs of local Chinese eateries and sleeping in any heated place he could find, including the backs of saloons.[13]

Sometimes unexpected good Samaritans would intervene and attempt to help some of these castaways. One well-known older woman in her fifties had worked quietly behind the scenes with some of these soiled doves in an effort to evacuate some of them out of the lifestyle and into other corners of the West.[14] But she was a rarity. Most residents of Deadwood were happy to use the town and the prostitutes if it suited their purposes, regardless of the consequences.

Another unusual aspect of Deadwood was the rather large contingent of Chinese residents, some of them prosperous merchants, who had ventured into the town and even set up a sort of Chinatown, supposedly the largest population of Chinese residents in any town the size of Deadwood in the United States. The Chinese operated various shops, hawking oriental goods that ranged from silks and embroideries to china, sandalwood, teak, and ivory. They were also operators of the ubiquitous Chinese laundries—so many of which operated that, "The clothes of Deadwood were as thoroughly washed as the gravel in the creek."[15] The Chinese often worked and saved their money in an effort to bring their relatives to Deadwood from China. When the leading Chinese merchant in Deadwood, Wing Tsue, brought his new wife over from China, he invited the wives of all his white friends to call on her at his home, and many did so. Young Estelline Bennett went with her mother and remembered that the home was

*heavily curtained and draped, richly furnished in teak and enamel, and the air was thick with the odor of sandalwood and Chinese punk. Mrs. Wing Tsue herself was the loveliest bit of exquisite china I ever saw. She was painted and mascaraed [sic] in a way no nice American woman could understand in those days but on her the effect was charming. Her black hair was built in a high pyramid with gorgeous pins and combs. Her brilliant silk jacket and trousers were heavy with embroidery and her tiny useless little feet were encased in embroidered satin shoes with wooden soles. She spoke no English but her gentle gracious manners and her courteous solicitude about the serving of tea and the delectable little almond cakes, small candied limes and other bonbons made us feel as if we had talked over all the polite topics of the day.*[16]

Other notable residents of Deadwood should also be mentioned, particularly one woman, as her name and Wild Bill's have often been linked, even romantically. As she herself recounted in her "autobiography": "My maiden name was Martha Cannary, was born in Princeton Missouri, May 2, 1852 . . . As a child I always had a fondness for adventure and out-door exercise and especial fondness for horses which I began to ride at an early age and continued to do so until I became an expert rider being able to ride the most vicious and stubborn horses, in fact the greater portion of my early times was spent in this manner."[17] So begins the self-told story of the famous or infamous Calamity Jane. She became a famed Western personality through her own invention of herself. Undoubtedly, many of the anecdotes and stories she told about herself were untrue or huge exaggerations, but she is still an interesting and notable figure in the Wild Bill saga.

Calamity's real claim to fame rested in her ability to do a man's work for a man's money. Her personal appearance was rough, and in the right sort of cowboy clothes, she could and did pass herself off as a man. This became very important for her survival, as there were simply not many professions open to women on the American frontier in the late 1880s and 1890s except schoolteacher and prostitute. She was neither. She was a unique commodity. She took great pride in her ability to pose as a male and do a male's work. As she said, describing a journey from Missouri to Montana in 1865:

*While on the way the greater portion of my time was spent in hunting along with the men and hunters of the party, in fact I was at all times with the men when there was excitement and adventures to be had.*

*By the time we reached Virginia City I was considered a remarkable good shot and a fearless rider for a girl of my age. I remember many occurrences on the journey from Missouri to Montana. Many time crossing the mountains of the trail were so bad that we frequently had to lower the wagons over ledges by hand with ropes for they were so rough and rugged that horses were of no use. We also had many exciting times fording streams for many of the streams in our way were noted for quick sands and boggy places, where unless we were very careful, we would have lost horses and all. Then we had many dangers to encounter in the way of streams swelling on account of heavy rains. On occasions of that kind then men would usually select the best places to cross the streams, myself on more than one occasion have mounted my pony and swam across the stream several times merely to amuse myself and have had many narrow escapes from having both myself and pony washed away to certain death, but as pioneers of those days had plenty of courage we overcame all obstacles and reached Virginia City in safety.*[18]

Calamity's narrative is not too different from other semi-truthful heroic literature written by pioneer adventurers and travelers. Most accounts of this type were written by men, attempting to pass themselves off as great heroes. Calamity Jane also claimed that she had been a scout for General Custer. This was where she supposedly began dressing as a man: "Joined General Custer as a scout at Fort Russell, Wyoming in 1870, and started for Arizona for the Indian campaign . . . When I joined Custer I donned the uniform of a soldier. It was a bit awkward at first, but I soon got to be perfectly at home in men's clothes"[19] She also claimed that she gained her unique nickname during one of her sojourns as a scout for the army:

*It was during this campaign that I was christened Calamity Jane. It was on Goose Creek, Wyoming where the town of Sheridan is now located. Captain Egan was in command of the post. We were ordered out to quell an uprising of the Indians, and were out for several days, had numerous skirmishes during which six of the soldiers were killed and several severely wounded. When on returning to the post we were ambushed about a mile and a half from our destination. When fired upon, Captain Egan was shot. I was riding in advance and on hearing the firing turned in my saddle and saw the Captain reeling in his saddle as though about to fall. I turned my horse and galloped back with all haste to his side and got there in time to catch him as he was falling. I lifted him onto my horse in front of me and succeeded in getting him safely to the fort. Captain Egan, on recovering, laughingly said, "I name you Calamity Jane, the heroine of the plains." I have borne that name up to the present time.[20]*

It has been persistently maintained by some writers and Old West storytellers that Calamity Jane and Wild Bill Hickok were lovers, however most historians believe that claim to be untrue, just another part of the myth of the Old West.[21] In fact, most contemporaries of Wild Bill and Calamity Jane were doubtful that a romantic liaison between them had taken place. White Eye Anderson, a friend of both, said in 1941:

*I don't believe it. Of course there were several years in which I did not know about Bill's doings, nor those of Jane. But I do know that when she came into our train at Fort Laramie, there was no friendship between Bill and her. She slept with Steve Utter, ate her meals with us and helped drink up Bill's whiskey. The last time I saw her was in October 1879 at Jack Bowman's ranch at Hat Creek. I was then leaving the Hills for Leadville. She was drinking at Jack's Bar and said, "Boys, I am married to George now, and am living a clean life." She was married to George Cosgrove . . .[22]*

Probably one of the most confusing things about Calamity's claims is that she reportedly requested that she be buried next to Wild Bill at Mount Moriah Cemetery in Deadwood. Although she died on August 1, 1903, the tombstone carvers changed the date to August 2. This way, her death would occur on the same date as the death of Wild Bill Hickok twenty-seven years earlier.[23]

Calamity Jane at Wild Bill's Grave, 1876. SOUTH DAKOTA STATE HISTORICAL SOCIETY

It seems unlikely that Calamity Jane and Wild Bill Hickok were anything more than acquaintances, perhaps extending as far as friendship. It seems, according to surviving correspondence between Wild Bill and his actual wife, Agnes Merman (Lake), that the two were very much in love, as demonstrated in the following letter written at around the time he would have supposedly been Calamity's lover:

*My own darling wife Agnes,*

*I have just a few minutes before this letter starts. I was never so well in my life; but you would laugh to see me now—just in from prospecting. Will go again tomorrow. Will write again in the morning, but God knows when the letter will start. My friend will take this to Cheyenne if he lives. I don't expect to hear from you, but it is all the same; I know my Agnes and only live to love her. Never mind, Pet, we will have a home yet, then we will be so happy. I am almost sure I will do well here. The man is hurrying me. Good bye dear wife.*

*Love to Emma,*
*J. B. Hickok.*[24]

Calamity Jane, late 1870s. SOUTH DAKOTA STATE HISTORICAL SOCIETY

Another prominent Deadwood resident with strong ties to Wild Bill was "Colorado Charly" Utter. Utter was many things, but he became a historical icon for a picture that supposedly showed him standing by Wild Bill's tombstone in Deadwood's cemetery and for having authored Wild Bill's epitaph.[25]

Most of what we think we know about Utter is probably fabricated from the same cloth as the Calamity Jane legend and from what we think we "know" about Hickok. As far as is known, Utter was born in 1838 in New York and made his way into Colorado Territory in his teens. He became known as a friend to Ute Indians and as an ever-diligent seeker of gold strikes. This would prove a key element in his later relations with Wild Bill in Deadwood. Utter had tried his hand at gold prospecting in Colorado, but ceased when the placer gold was exhausted. He spent at least one winter in the Rockies, living as a true mountain man, hunting for food and living in a log cabin. He became known for his mountaineering skills and abilities. The *Daily Miner's Register* noted, "Charley is probably the best mountaineer in the territory, and we regard his authority concerning the passes as perfectly reliable."[26]

Utter also got into the saloon business, as the same newspaper noted thirty days later: "Charley Utter is proprietor of a neat and elegant billiard hall at Empire City. His place has been open but a few days, and yet his drawer is reported to be weighty with greenbacks already."[27]

Utter was also known as a generous person to those in need. During winter weather, a group of Colorado Territory government officials were rescued by Utter when they were caught in a blizzard. The group stayed with him for fifteen days, until the storm passed and they recovered. They wrote of his generosity and kindness—at one point he ventured out to find some horses for his guests. Utter then became involved in the freighting/saddle pack business, as reported by the *Rocky Mountain News*: "Charley Utter informs us that he has made arrangements to run a regular saddle and pack train during the present summer from Empire City, over the Berthoud Pass and through the Middle Park to the great hot soda springs. Saddle horses can be obtained anytime, and trains of pack animals will leave every few days."[28] Utter also found time to serve as a guide for various hunting and exploring parties, including one made up of dignitaries such as Secretary Frank Hall (if Colorado had been state and not a territory, his office would have been governor). This trip proved difficult, as one of the guests suffered a seizure while on the trail and it proved very difficult to transport him back to civilization. Utter once again showed his mettle and inventiveness, however, by constructing a litter and retrieving the ailing man back to town. He also spent some time recovering from a self-inflicted gunshot wound to his abdomen suffered while out on another of his favorite side expeditions—prospecting.[29] Utter married in 1866, and this seems to have quieted some of his more adventurous tendencies.

He didn't need to venture far to find adventure, as his pack-train business was booming thanks to the increasing activities of the mining companies in the area. One visitor who stayed the night with the Utters had this observation: "Lodged for the night with that princely young mountaineer Charley Utter. Charley has a pack train engaged in conveying a ton of ore a day from the Anglo-Saxon mine to Johnson's furnace . . . The animals are making two trips a day."[30] Utter also obtained the contract for the delivery of the mail, which he simply put on his pack trains that were delivering ore. His brother and sister-in-law eventually came to Colorado and settled near Charley and his wife, and all seemed well for familial happiness. Utter, a lifelong teetotaler, and his wife became involved in the local temperance movement. It is almost unimaginable that a close friend of Wild Bill was a teetotaler, but such was the case with Charley Utter![31]

Utter's fondness for gold strikes and pack trains led him to explore the Black Hills with his most famous acquaintance, Wild Bill, in 1876. Utter became a leading supplier of the various mining enterprises in the Black Hills through his pack-saddle business. His mules delivered prodigious amounts of supplies to the hungry prospectors, including 37,500 pounds of flour. The inventive and entrepreneurial Utter also organized a mail-delivery company modeled on the Pony Express to help the miners get their mail. Utter's first recorded activity with Hickok occurred when Hickok decided to leave Cheyenne, Wyoming, and enter the Black Hills in search of gold. Hickok joined one of Utter's pack trains and left

Cheyenne on June 27, 1876, for the Black Hills. Accompanying Utter and Hickok was Charley's brother, Steve.[32]

Hickok's party passed by a ranch owned by John Hunton on their way into the Black Hills and the goldfields. Hunton mentioned the moment in his diary:

*On June 30 1876, "Bill" and a party of men who were on their way to the Black Hills mines, traveling with a four horse team and wagon, camped about two miles south of my ranch. The next morning they passed my place and "Bill" stopped long enough to say "How." He then said, "So long Jack" and went away. A few hours afterward Waddie S. Bacom, one of my men who had been out riding, came in and said: "Mr. Hunton, I met a man down the road who said he was 'Wild Bill' and wanted you to go to the place he camped last night and get his cane which he stuck in the ground at his head where he made his bed last night in the edge of a patch of bushes, and send it to him at Deadwood, by someone you can trust to deliver it to him. Be sure not to send it except by some mutual friend whom you both know, as he did not want any chance of losing it." I sent the man for the cane, and he brought it to me. In less than a month I heard of Bill's death . . . I kept the cane until 1921 and then gave it to Miss Eunice G. Anderson, State Historian, to be deposited in the museum of the Wyoming Historical Society, where it is now deposited and can be seen.*[33]

Hickok's arrival in Deadwood was also recounted by Harry Young, a barkeeper who had been a friend to Hickok in Hays City and renewed the association in Deadwood:

*About the middle of June there arrived in Deadwood my old friend Charlie Utter, commonly known as Colorado Charlie. They were mounted, and a more picturesque sight could not be imagined than Wild Bill on horseback. This character had never been north of Cheyenne before this. Many in Deadwood knew him; many knew him only by reputation, particularly those who came from Montana . . .*

*They rode up to the saloon where I was working, both of them having known Carl Mann before. He being a great friend of Bill's they naturally called on him first. They dismounted and walked into the saloon, great crowds following them, until the room was packed.*

*Mann cordially invited them, asking them to make his saloon their headquarters, which they agreed to do. This meant money to Mann, as Bill would be a great drawing card.*[34]

All of them settled into Deadwood as permanent residents. Utter began his pony express service between the claims and settlements of the Black Hills, and Wild Bill sat in on many poker games. One member of the Utter saddle-pack train who accompanied Wild Bill and Colorado Charley to Deadwood from Cheyenne was White Eye Anderson, who late in life made these observations on the trip:

*When my brother Charlie and I arrived in Cheyenne in June 1876 to go to Deadwood, we went over to the Elephant feed corral to see if we could find a conveyance to take us there. There we met Charlie Utter and Wild Bill.*

*It had been several years since I had seen Bill, but he recognized me at once, held out his hand and said, "Touch flesh my boy." This was an old time invitation he always used, to shake hands. He then told Colorado Charlie about me, and it was this friendship with Wild Bill that caused Charlie to say that my brother and I could travel with them . . . I always felt safe when Wild Bill was around and was a little bit stuck on myself. He would introduce me to men he knew and would always say, "This is my friend, the White-Eyed kid" . . . Wild Bill liked to play poker and faro and he was always playing cards. He told me to leave them alone as I was not smart enough to beat the game in a showdown. Bill didn't talk much but he always said something important. His eyes were weak, he could see pretty well in the daytime, but at night when he went somewhere he always asked me to go with him. He was over six feet tall, very broad in the shoulders and narrow in the waist. I think the reason he was so narrow in the waist was that he always had on his belt with two six-shooters and did not give his belly a chance to grow. He had brown hair, not very thick, and he shaved smooth all but his moustache, which was long. His eyes were kind of bluish steel grey, and when he looked at you he could tell exactly what you were thinking, and I believe that was why he was such a good poker player, I think he could tell just by looking at a man what kind of hand he held.*[35]

Wild Bill's reputed residence in Deadwood, circa 1876–1877. Identity of the figures is unknown. SOUTH DAKOTA STATE HISTORICAL SOCIETY

Hickok's marksmanship was also commented on by Anderson, who seems to have hero-worshiped Wild Bill. According to Anderson, however, the rumors of Bill's sight loss during his time with Cody were accurate:

*Wild Bill's sight was practically gone when I knew him, and he could hardly see at all in darkness. I used to bring him back to camp after he had played poker. Some of the boys said he was "moon-blind." But every morning he was at target practice. His shooting was all done at 25 paces, and at that distance he could see perfectly, and never missed a shot at anything. He did not take aim at all. I have never seen him take aim when shooting at a target. He always carried his guns butts forward, as did all western men, especially gunmen. He often drew both guns at once and fired simultaneously. It was a simple twist of the wrist to bring out the guns when carried butts forward, and they came upward instead of having to come backward to clear the holster as "bad men" do in the movies. Wild Bill had his old buffalo rifle . . . it was a .56 caliber Springfield with three bands on the stock, called a needle gun. At this time he had discarded the Colt Navy cap and ball pistols, and had two of latest Colt .38 caliber cartridge six-shooters. The triggers were filed off and the hammers filed smooth, so that his thumbs would slip off easily. He had a whole case of cartridges and often used to practice, about every day. He liked these pistols much better than he had the old .44's used in earlier years, and kept them brand new . . . My old hat was full of holes where Wild Bill would shoot at it when I threw it into the air. He would always say, after shooting, "Count the holes, my boy, and see if they total up to the shots fired. If they don't, then I'd better quit." He shot equally well with either hand, or both at the same time, and the holes always "totaled up." He bought me a new hat when we got to Deadwood, paid fifty dollars for it and said, "My boy, don't let anybody shoot at it; fifty dollars is too much money . . .*[36]

Once Hickok had actually arrived in Deadwood, he became the subject of a number of interesting tales and accounts. One of the most famous involved his confrontation with six Montana gunmen who dreaded the thought that perhaps Hickok had come to Deadwood to assume a law enforcement position and "clean up" the crooked gambling and devious dealings that were the standard play in town. According to the story, Hickok was informed by his good friend Charlie Utter that six Montana gunmen had made a public threat against him—to the effect that he would be killed in the next few hours. Supposedly Hickok coolly checked and rechecked his pistols and went to the saloon where the would-be assassins were known to reside. "I understand that you cheap, would be gun fighters from Montana have been making remarks about me. I want you to understand unless they are stopped there will shortly be a number of cheap funerals in Deadwood. I have come to this town, not to court notoriety, but to live in peace, and do not propose to stand for your insults." Wild Bill then ordered the men to disarm and give him their weapons. They did so and Hickok backed out of the saloon The local miners who had been hoping to see Hickok blow the six men out the back of the saloon were disappointed, but they let off steam by harassing and heckling the humbled Montana gunmen as they left the saloon and followed Hickok out to the street.[37]

Other stories supposedly related by Hickok during his tenure in Deadwood were clearly designed as gags to play on his fame and the people's willingness to accept virtually anything he said as rock-solid truth. He had a wry sense of humor, which the following story illustrates. Hickok spent a good deal of time in the saloons, particularly the tavern of Harry Young. Young said that Wild Bill told him that once when he was scouting for Custer he found an opening in a cliff two feet wide and ten feet long. He promptly explored the small area and found himself thinking that it would provide great protection from Indians, when suddenly he saw an Indian entering the opening and coming toward him. Bill claimed that he was armed with one pistol and had only six shots plus his knife. He then said that he promptly shot the Indian and then another one came and then another. He shot each one in succession until he had exhausted his six shots, then he drew his knife and backed up against the wall in the far end of the cavern. At this point Wild Bill would stop relating the story until one of the listeners asked him what happened next. Hickok would reply that he didn't have many options, as there were so many Indians and he had only a knife. When another listener asked him what he did next, "By God, they killed me boys!" was Bill's reply. Eventually everyone caught on to the joke and general merriment ensued.[38]

Another story Hickok told at about the same time involved a gold-eating snake. He said he was in Colorado riding his horse one day when he looked back and saw a huge fifty-foot-long snake with a head of a man following him. In his tale, he tried to outrun this beast but found it impossible, so he turned in the saddle and shot it dead. He leaped from his horse and cut the animal open with his knife and found lodged in its stomach gold dust amounting to $875. He then claimed that he buried the snake and took the dust into a nearby town, and this led to the gold rush in Colorado. According to Wild Bill, the gold-eating snake should have received the credit for the first strike. This story was also received with great glee by his listeners.[39]

Although known for telling humorous stories about himself, Hickok also displayed a serious, even morose side during his short time in Deadwood. His good friend Charlie Utter claimed that when the group first entered the Deadwood Gulch, Bill supposedly said to Utter, "I have a hunch that I am in my last camp and will never leave this gulch alive." Utter told him that he was dreaming, but Hickok continued, "No I am not dreaming. Something tells me that my time is up, but where it is coming from I do not know, as I cannot think of one living enemy who would wish to kill me."[40] Also, on the night before his death, he told another friend, when asked why he seemed so downcast that, ". . . I have a presentiment that my time is up and that I am soon to be killed." Later that same night he wrote a letter to Agnes, who was staying with relatives in Ohio, conveying some of these feelings: "Agnes Darling, If such should be we never meet again, while firing my last shot, I will gently breathe the name of my wife—Agnes—and with wishes even for my enemies I will make the plunge and try to swim to the other shore."[41] In another presentiment of doom, Hickok was quoted in a news story after his death supposedly discussing his coming demise: "A week before Wild Bill's death he was heard to remark to a friend, 'I feel that my days are numbered; my sun is sinking fast; I know I shall be killed here, something tells me I shall never leave these hills alive; somebody is going to kill me.

But I don't know who it is or why he is going to do it. I have killed many men in my day, but I never killed a man yet but what it was kill or get killed with me. But I have two trusty friends, one is my six shooter and the other is California Joe.'"[42] This soliloquy is difficult to believe. Surely Hickok would not have been surprised that there were literally dozens of friends and relatives of men he killed who would have welcomed a chance at revenge against him. Also, by that time he was well aware that the notoriety of his name had invited all sorts of would be gunslingers to "test" themselves against the legendary Wild Bill.

Other accounts of Hickok's last days do not mention any premonitions on his part, but seem to show the same old Wild Bill. Leander Richardson would write for *Scribner's* in the months after Bill's death:

> *I had been in town only a few moments when I met Charlie Utter, better known as Colorado Charley to whom I had a letter of introduction, and who at once invited me to share his camp while I remained in the region. On our way over to his tent, we met J. B. Hickok, "Wild Bill" the hero of a hundred battles. Bill was Utter's "pardner" and I was introduced at once. Of course I had heard of him, the greatest scout of the West, but I was not prepared to find such a man as he proved to be. Most of the western scouts do not amount to much. They do a great deal in the personal reminiscences way, but otherwise they are generally of the class described as frauds. In "Wild Bill" I found a man who talked little and had done a great deal. He was about six feet two inches in height and very powerfully built; his face was intelligent, his hair blonde and falling in ringlets upon his broad shoulders; his eyes, blue and pleasant, looked one straight in the face when he talked; and his lips, thin and compressed, were only partly hidden by a straw colored moustache. His costume was a curiously blended union of the habiliments of the borderman and the drapery of the fashionable dandy. Beneath the skirts of his elaborately embroidered buckskin coat gleamed the handles of two silver-mounted revolvers, which were his constant companions. His voice was low and musical, but through its hesitation I could catch a ring of self-reliance and consciousness of strength. Yet he was the most courteous man I had met on the plains.*

*On the following day I asked to see him use a pistol and he assented. At his request I tossed a tomato can about 15 feet into the air, both his pistols being in his belt when it left my hand. He drew one of them, and fired two bullets through the tin can before it struck the ground. Then he followed it along, firing as he went, until both weapons were empty. You have heard the expression "quick as lightning"? Well, that will describe "Wild Bill." He was noted all over the country for rapidity of motion, courage, and certainty of aim. Wherever he went he controlled the people around him, and many a quarrel has been ended by his simple announcement, "This has gone far enough."*[43]

Interestingly this recollection seems to contradict the other accounts of Hickok as someone who was "wearing out" with bad eyesight and loss of nerve. It is difficult to say which is the true tale, but, in any case, his days were numbered.

# CHAPTER 11

# Trials and Consequences

HICKOK AND HIS PARTNER CHARLIE UTTER HAD SEVERAL CLAIMS THEY worked in the area around Deadwood, but it was extremely hot in August 1876, and Utter and Hickok tended to work their claims in the morning and then spend the hotter afternoon hours in the shade of a saloon, often playing cards. Hickok frequented a game at the Number 10 saloon, where Harry Young—an old friend from Hays City—tended bar. Hickok often stopped to talk with Young before assuming his seat at the card table.

Hickok played several games with an assortment of players on August 1, 1876. When a Captain Massie, a retired steamboat captain from the Missouri and Mississippi River trade, left the table, a bystander named Jack McCall took his place.[1] McCall's history is difficult to pin down. Some sources give his birthplace as Kentucky, but others claim it was New Orleans. He had many aliases, and he was going by the name Bill Sutherland in 1876. But he had been previously known as Curly Jack and also as Buffalo Curly. Only one picture of McCall is thought to exist, but authorities are unsure of its authenticity.[2] McCall was essentially a loser who became famous despite his poor performance in the game of life.

On August 2, 1876, the day after McCall and Hickok met over cards the first time, Hickok decided to enter Number 10 in the afternoon for his usual game of cards. When he arrived at three o'clock, Hickok greeted Harry Young and then sat down at a game featuring Carl Mann (owner of the saloon), Charles Rich, and Captain Massie at Mann's invitation. Hickok usually liked to sit with his back to the wall, the typical place for anyone with an enemy or enemies. That afternoon, however, Hickok's wall seat was occupied by Rich, and Hickok's request for a trade was not taken seriously by anyone at the table. The other players apparently did not believe that anyone would really attempt a deadly strike on the now-retired law enforcement legend.

From the seat he took at the table, Wild Bill was able to face the front door, but there was a smaller door in the rear of the saloon that Hickok knew he could not see. Hickok's luck was poor that afternoon, and he had to request fifteen dollars' worth of pocket checks from Harry Young at the bar. At about four o'clock, Charlie Utter, who had been sitting near Hickok for a time, departed for a meal. At that point, Jack McCall entered Number 10. He came in by the front door and was apparently ignored by everyone in the saloon. McCall managed to make his way along the length of the bar until he was behind Hickok's chair. Hickok is supposed to have declared to Massie that he had gone broke on the last hand. Then suddenly there was a loud explosion of a pistol discharging and Wild Bill's head jerked forward, propelled by the blast of McCall's pistol. The initial reaction from everyone was stunned silence as McCall moved quickly toward the open rear door. After attempting to fire his pistol at Harry Young and another man, McCall ran out the back of the saloon and jumped on a horse. The saddle cinch was loose, however, and McCall tumbled from his mount. He then ran into a nearby butcher shop and tried to hide, but was quickly discovered and forced to come out at gunpoint.

A coroner examined Hickok's fatal wound, noting that the path of the projectile went from "the base of the brain, a little to the right of center, passing through in a straight line, making its exit through the right cheek between the upper and lower jaw bones, loosening several of the molar teeth in its passage, and carrying a portion of the cerebellum through the wound. From the nature of the wound death must necessarily have been instantaneous."[3] Doc Pierce, the town's barber, and also a sort of medical man, served as the de-facto undertaker and described the situation in a 1920s letter to Hickok biographer Frank Wilstach as follows:

*When they unlocked the door for me to get to his body, he was lying on his side, with his knees drawn up just as he slid off his stool. We had no chairs in those days—and his fingers were still crimped from holding his poker hand. Charlie Rich, who sat beside him, said he never saw a muscle move. Bill's hand read "aces and eights"—two pair, and since that day aces and eights have been known as "the dead man's hand" in the Western country. It seemed like fate, Bill's taking off. Of the murderer's big Colt 45 six gun, every chamber loaded, the cartridge that killed Bill was the only one that would fire. What would have been McCall's chances if he had snapped one of the other cartridges when he sneaked up and held his gun to Bill's head? He would now be known as No. 37 on the file list of Mr. Hickok."*[4]

Doc Pierce also described Wild Bill in death: "When Bill was shot through the head he bled out quickly, and when he was laid out he looked like a wax figure. I have seen many dead men on the field of battle and in civil life, but Wild Bill was the prettiest corpse I have ever seen. His long moustache was attractive, even in death, and his long tapering fingers looked like marble."[5]

The inevitable arrangements were made for a funeral and burial and recollected by White Eye Anderson:

*When Bill was killed the doors of No. 10 were locked up . . . A barber named or called "Doc" was with the men who came to camp. Mr. Rutherford had a one-horse express wagon, and they sent him with it to the saloon, and he brought Bill's body back to our camp. Doc and the two Charlies took Bill's boots off and Doc fixed up the body in good shape. A carpenter made Bill's coffin out of rough pine lumber, covering it in black cloth on the outside, and lining it with white cloth, and it looked pretty good for a home-made coffin. He laid there that night, and I sat up and watched the coffin to see that nothing bothered it. The next day, in the afternoon, Mr. Rutherford with his little wagon brought the body to the grave we had dug.*[6]

A newspaper correspondent also described Wild Bill's body:

*In a handsome coffin covered with black cloth and richly mounted with silver ornaments, lay Wild Bill, a picture of perfect repose. His long chestnut hair, evenly parted over his marble brow, hung in waving ringlets over the broad shoulders; his face was cleanly shaved except the drooping moustache, which shaded a mouth in death almost seemed to smile, but which in life was unusually grave; the arms were folded over the still breast, which inclosed a heart which had beat with regular pulsations in the most startling scenes of blood and violence. The corpse was clad in complete dress-suit of black broadcloth, new underclothing, and white linen shirt; beside him in the coffin lay his trusty rifle, which the deceased prized above all other things, and which was to be buried with him in compliance with an expressed desire.*[7]

Hickok's close friend, Colorado Charlie, posted a notice using the equipment of the local newspaper, the *Black Hills Pioneer*, stating, "Died, in Deadwood, Black Hills, August 2 1876, from the effect of a pistol shot, J. B. Hickok, (Wild Bill) formerly of Cheyenne, Wyoming. Funeral services will be held at Charlie Utter's camp, on Thursday afternoon, August 3, 1876 at 3 o'clock. All are respectfully invited to attend."[8]

Meanwhile, arrangements were also made for a trial for the killer, Jack McCall. A coroner's jury was also empaneled, with C. H. Sheldon as foreman, to examine the body and consider the circumstances of the shooting. After the coroner's jury delivered its verdict, which confirmed that Hickok was shot through the head and died instantly, arrangements were made for the actual trial of McCall on August 3, 1876. The proceedings were held at McDaniel's theatre in Deadwood. Since Deadwood was essentially an illegal settlement, as it was located on Indian lands in the Black Hills, no regular court officers were in existence, therefore it was a self-constituted court that attempted to adjudicate the murder. Pro Tempore Judge W. L. Kuykendall was chosen to preside over McCall's trial. He would later describe the situation in his book:

*To observe the proper formalities, I was selected to act as chairman. After stating the object of the meeting to be the organization of a second miner's court to try the case the next day, I stated that if any man present were not in harmony with the movement then was the time for him to leave. All remained. It was decided the jury should be*

Interior of Saloon #10, circa 1940. SOUTH DAKOTA STATE HISTORICAL SOCIETY

*selected by making out a list of twenty names of miners from each of the three mining districts, the name of each to be written on a separate slip of paper and well shaken in a hat, the twelve drawn there from to be the jury, lists to be made by a committee to be selected by the meeting when court convened next morning. On motion I was elected Judge, Isaac Brown, Sheriff, John Swift, clerk, Colonel May, Prosecuting Attorney, and Judge Miller, attorney for the prisoner. Both were able lawyers at that time, although without clients, for there was no law in force then or for month's afterwards.[9]*

Wild Bill's grave in Deadwood, South Dakota. The statue has since been replaced with a bronze bust. SOUTH DAKOTA STATE HISTORICAL SOCIETY

A trial held under these circumstances, especially in light of Kuykendall's last statement (". . . for there was no law in force then or for month's afterwards") could not possibly have been legal. It is certainly a reflection on the poor jurisprudence then available in Dakota Territory, as well as in the illegal settlement of Deadwood, that Jack McCall's first trial ever took place at all.

Wild Bill's biographer, J. W. Buel, however, offers a slightly different story than Judge Kuykendall. Buel noted that Colonel May was chosen as the prosecutor and that McCall selected A. B. Chapline as his defense counsel. When Chapline was unable to attend due to illness, another local judge, a Judge Miller, was chosen to represent McCall. Three men (Mr. Reid, Jos. Harringrton, and Mr. Cain) were then appointed to select a jury of twelve from the names of thirty-three residents from their respective districts. The preparations for the trial caused great excitement in Deadwood, and there was some talk of a lynching before the trial, but this was avoided and the trial commenced on August 3, 1876.[10]

The jury was selected and was made up of John Mann, J. J. Bumfs, L. D. Brokow, Edward Burke, L. A. Judd, J. H. Thompson, Charles Whitehead, John E. Thompson, Geo. S. Hopkins, K. F. Towle, J. F. Cooper, and Alexander Travis.[11] After the jury was sworn in, the trial began. Several witnesses were examined including Charles Rich, Carl Mann, Samuel Young, George Shingle, Isaac Brown, Pat Smith, H. H. Pitkins, and Ira Ford. A newspaper reporter from a Chicago paper described the defendant's appearance in court:

> *Never did a more forbidding countenance face a court than that of Jack McCall. His head, which is covered by a thick crop of chestnut hair, is very narrow as to the parts occupied by the intellectual portion of the brain, while the animal development is exceedingly large. A small, sandy moustache covers a sensual mouth. The nose is what is commonly called "snub," cross eyes, and a florid complexion and the picture is finished. He was clad in a blue flannel shirt, brown overalls, heavy shoes, and as he sat in a stooping position with his arms folded across his breast, he evidently assumed a nonchalance and bravado which was foreign to his feelings and betrayed by the spasmodic heavings of his heart.*[12]

During the proceedings McCall himself was asked if he wished to make a statement on his own behalf, and he indicated that he would prefer to do so, offering a version of the shooting that would become a part of the legend of the West. McCall addressed the court: "Yes, I have a few words to say. Well men, I have but few words to say. Wild Bill killed my brother, and I killed him. Wild Bill threatened to kill me if I ever crossed his path. I am not sorry for what I done; if I had to, I would do the same thing over again."

Judge Miller played off of McCall's contention of brotherly vengeance—regardless of its veracity. Miller called upon the feelings of the jury:

*Men, comrades, you have been chosen to decide the guilt and punish-*
*ment of one of your own companions; look upon the honest counte-*
*nance of this poor boy who is being tried for his life because he struck*
*down the assassin of a dearly beloved brother; note particularly, that*
*unflinching and innocent eye, which could not possibly belong to a*
*man who could do anything wrong.*[13]

The prosecutor closed his remarks with a recitation of the facts of the
case and offered his view of the motive: "If this be not murder then there
never was murder committed. The deceased in his bloody winding-sheet,
from his mountain grave, demanded that a proper punishment be meted
out to his villainous assassin." He also noted the unusual fact that, "It
is strange if the prisoner has been living for years with a sworn deter-
mination to kill Wild Bill, that only two days ago he should have been
pleasantly engaged playing cards with him."[14]

After both camps presented their closing statements, at about six
o'clock that evening, the case was given to the jury, and they returned a
verdict at nine o'clock that evening. Initially eleven jurors were for acquittal and only one for conviction. It was first proposed that McCall be fined
twenty dollars (!) and be released, or be held in jail until the fine was
paid. This proposal is certainly a reflection on the value of human life in
Deadwood—apparently it was worth twenty dollars. A further hour and
thirty minutes of deliberations followed, and it was eventually decided
upon to simply declare McCall innocent of all charges and release him.
Apparently, upon further discussion, human life was not even worth
twenty dollars.[15]

Thus, perhaps the greatest gunman in American history was assassi-
nated by a back-shooter during a card game who got away with it.

## Chapter 12

# Aftermath

ONE MYSTERIOUS ASPECT OF THE ACQUITTAL OF JACK MCCALL IS THE question as to why none of Hickok's friends sought immediate revenge on the killer of Wild Bill. Charlie Utter would have been the obvious candidate to take on the murderer of his friend and partner, but he apparently stopped short of actual violence. Hickok's friend, California Joe, almost terminated McCall but didn't take things that far. According to the August 26, 1876, issue of the *Daily Leader*, the following occurred shortly after the not guilty verdict was delivered:

> *Could California Joe have arrived in time, no doubt McCall would have been hanged; but he was down at Crook City, looking for Indians . . . Joe came to Deadwood, and after hearing all the particulars of the killing of Wild Bill, walked down to McCall's cabin, and calling him out asked him if he didn't think the air about there was rather light for him. McCall's cheeks blanched, and he feebly answered he thought it was. "Well, I guess you had better take a walk then," said Joe, and seating himself on the side of the hill he watched the retreating figure out of sight.*[1]

One can imagine what the result would have been if it had been reversed and Hickok was left with a dead friend who had been murdered by a back-shooting coward. That individual's life span could have been measured in minutes.

Even though Hickok had not maintained close connections with his wife and family back East, his death was still a great shock to them, particularly the way it occurred. Hickok's sister Lydia would recall in an 1896 article:

*I remember the day the paper came with the news of Bill's murder . . . Mother had been a sufferer from inflammatory rheumatism for two years before that, and had not taken a step for eighteen months. My sister was standing at the gate when a neighbor came by and brought the Chicago paper giving an account of Bill's death. He handed it to my sister. She took it and saw the headlines, but did not read all of it. She folded it up and hurried into the house, hiding the paper in the kitchen behind a mirror on a shelf. Then, composing herself, she went in where mother was sitting. "Mother," she said, "I am going over to the store a minute, and will be right back." She put on her bonnet and ran to the little store about two hundred yards away to tell . . . one of my brothers. They all came back to the house together. When they entered the sitting room there sat mother, the newspaper lying at her side, slowly rocking back and forth, while the blood from a hemorrhage of the lungs dyed the front of her light dress. "I saw you get the paper Linda," she said to my sister, "and when you did not bring it in I knew what was in it, so I went to get it." She never fully recovered from it and she died two years later still mourning over Bill's terrible death.*[2]

If instead of going to Deadwood, Hickok had returned home to live near his relations in a peaceful area far from the bloody saloons and dives with which he was so familiar, perhaps he could have lived his days out in peace and quiet and avoided the violent death that had often been forecasted for him by various newspaperman and opposing gunmen. On the other hand, he still would have been Wild Bill Hickok and sooner or later, perhaps, some up-and-coming murdering outlaw or gunman would have heard about his residency and sought him out in an effort to win immortality as the killer of Wild Bill. Hickok was not a peaceable man, and he probably would not have lasted long rocking on the porch in the small community where his family resided. He had been exposed to numerous adrenaline-pumping encounters where his life was on the line and he had found a way out of all of them through his gunnery skills and his wits. It is likely that life back East would have simply been too tame for him.

As for Jack McCall, after California Joe sent him packing, he should have sneaked out of town and made his way somewhere where he could have remained anonymous.

Unfortunately for McCall, his own nature proved to be his worst enemy. After the acquittal, McCall lingered around Deadwood for several days but eventually left town and was seen exiting the environs of Deadwood by several residents. He was destitute, and he made his way to Julesberg, Colorado, where he inquired about work and found employment with a saloon keeper who was also the owner of a large and well-known ranch near the town. The saloon keeper was in the midst of harvesting his yearly crops, so McCall and several other employees were sent to work in the fields. The saloon keeper seems to have been a very generous employer, as he prepared a huge feast for his hired hands as a way to compensate them for their hard field work. It was a great surprise to the saloon keeper then, when McCall was not to be found the next day when work began again. In fact McCall had not only left his employer, he had also relieved him of his horse and saddle and a generous amount of provisions.[3] McCall made his way to Wyoming, where he apparently thought he was beyond the reach of any law or justice for Wild Bill's murder.

However, McCall was unable to remain silent about his murder of a Western superstar. McCall apparently concluded that he had been acquitted by a legitimate court of law and "gotten away with murder." Indeed, far from being reticent to discuss the killing, McCall took the opportunity to discuss his role in the murder with a reporter from a Laramie, Wyoming, newspaper, who wrote:

> *McCall [and this we believe to be his real name] is a medium sized man, and wears a light moustache. His brown eyes are slightly crossed, and restless, and he has an impediment in his speech. His manner is nervous and he shows every symptom of possessing an uneasy conscience. He is careful to always have the wall at his back when in*

*conversation, as though afraid of being shot unawares. His story as related by himself is as follows:*

*"When I first met Wild Bill in Deadwood he asked me if I was not from Fort Hayes [sic] Kansas, but I answered 'No,' although I had seen Bill in Hayes, and easily recognized him in Deadwood as the man who killed my brother. At the time I shot him I was employed in carrying the mail from Red Cloud to Deadwood, a job which no one else would undertake. On the day of the shooting I had a dispute with Bill about some gold dust which he had as good as robbed me of in a poker game.*

*"We quarreled some time about it and I finally slapped his face. He only laughed and said 'that is alright.' Between three and four o'clock the next afternoon I went into the Cricket saloon, where Bill and a party of men were playing cards, and after walking up and down a few times, stepped up to Bill, and telling him to 'look out,' shot him, the ball entered at his ear. When I warned him he smiled but made no effort to resist or protect himself. I cocked my revolver and snapped it at the men he was playing with, but the d-nd thing wouldn't go, although the cylinder turned. I rushed out of the saloon, mounted a horse standing near, and started off, but the saddle was loose and turned with me, so I was forced to surrender to a crowd of several hundred men. I was arrested, lodged in jail and guarded by 25 armed men.*

*"Great excitement prevailed and I fully expected to be lynched, but another excitement caused by a Mexican bringing into town the head of an Indian diverted attention from me and preparations were made for a trial. I employed Counsel, the trial was conducted in regular form, and I was acquitted. Soon afterwards I left Deadwood, came to Cheyenne and went from there to Laramie, where I arrived Monday evening. I lost $700 here that night and think the thieves will be caught. I have three gold claims near Deadwood and was intending to stay there this Winter."*

*This is the story of the murderer, substantially as told by himself and we submit it to our readers as related. We are of the opinion that a Dakota judge and jury will give the man a full and fair trial, and that he will be meted out just punishment for his crime. Wild Bill had few friends, but he did not, in our opinion, deserve a dog's death, and if as one witness will testify today, his murderer has stated that Bill never killed a brother of his, and (if) this can be proven it will go hard for McCall, and the gallows will undoubtedly receive him.*[4]

There are number of unbelievable things contained in this story, including McCall's assertion that he had slapped Wild Bill's face and Bill only laughed in response. It is very unlikely that any human being who did this would have remained alive, let alone elicited a laugh from Hickok. McCall also asserted that Hickok apparently saw McCall prepare his shot and showed no resistance to it. This also contradicts all eyewitness testimony, which clearly showed that McCall was scared to death and did not engage with Hickok until he was sure Wild Bill had paid him no notice so there was no danger of entering a real "shoot-out" with Wild Bill, which undoubtedly would have cost McCall his life.

Apparently others also doubted McCall's version of events. Several Wyoming area newspapers reported that, among other things, McCall confessed to a judge (Judge Blair) in Laramie that he was indeed guilty of the murder of Wild Bill. Further, a witness to a confession by McCall told another reporter that McCall told him that Wild Bill never killed McCall's brother and in fact the issue in contention between him and Hickok involved an argument over cards. It was also asserted that perhaps McCall had killed another man—or at least robbed him—directly after his acquittal, as he was seen with a new gold watch and chain and a large sum of money, but when he was on trial he only possessed forty-three dollars.[5]

McCall's freedom was eventually placed in peril because of his statements and his own actions. Colonel May, the prosecutor of McCall at the illegal trial previously held in Deadwood, had, unbeknownst to McCall, followed him to Wyoming. May heard about McCall's boasting, and he reported these statements to the legal authorities. Subsequently, a warrant was issued for McCall's arrest and he was arrested by Deputy US Marshal Balcombe on August 29, 1876, less than a month after the murder and McCall's trial in Deadwood. McCall was first removed to Cheyenne, where he appeared before US Commissioner Brunner, who was awaiting an order from the governor of Dakota Territory for McCall's move to Yankton, Dakota Territory, for a new trial.

While being held in Laramie, McCall appeared before Judge Blair, who allowed McCall a defense counsel, C. W. Bramel. The prosecutor was General Jenkins. Two witnesses, George Shingle and Louis Meize, both testified to the effect that McCall was indeed the murderer of Hickok. Most damaging, however, was McCall's confession to Judge Blair that he did indeed kill Wild Bill, thus negating his rights against self-incrimination.[6] One wonders if he was so proud of his deed that he believed his fame as Hickok's killer would preclude him from paying for what was obviously a cowardly act of murder. On the basis of his confession, McCall was sent by Judge Blair to Yankton for trial, as the original trial in Deadwood was extra-legal in that it was not officially sanctioned by the territorial government.

As the new trial date approached, warrants were issued for the appearance of witnesses, including Captain Massie, one of Hickok's poker companions on the day of his murder, who was ordered to appear at the Yankton trial as a witness for the prosecution. Massie supposedly carried in his wrist the ball that had been shot into Wild Bill's head. It had passed through Hickok's head and entered Massie's arm. Some sources claim that Massie bore this bullet until his dying day, however Buel wrote: "The ball went crashing through the back of Bill's head and came out at the center of his right cheek; but before it had spent its force it struck Capt. Massey [sic] in the left arm, shivering the bone, and was so firmly embedded that it had to be cut out."[7] Bullet or not, Massie was ordered to attend the trial.

McCall was duly indicted for murder in Yankton on October 18, 1876. He stated that Jack McCall was his real name, and he entered a not-guilty plea. The judge in the trial was an assistant justice of the territorial supreme court, Grenville Bennett, who appointed General W. W. Beadle as McCall's defense counsel. McCall tried to introduce a motion to delay the trial so he could gather witnesses for his defense, but this motion was denied on October 19.[8] On October 20, George Shingle was ordered to appear for the prosecution at the Yankton courthouse. Preparations for McCall's trial appeared to be taking the proper shape. Then, on November 9, McCall, apparently deciding that his legal "goose was cooked," decided to attempt a jail break. McCall and his "cellie" a man named McCarty, attacked their jailer, J. B. Robertson, and were narrowly prevented from making a break for freedom by the timely intervention of Marshal Burdick and one of his assistants, who reportedly stopped the would be jail-breakers by poking them with their pistols.[9] At that point McCall apparently decided that he would rather face the jury than the marshal's loaded pistol. Perhaps he thought a small chance was better than no chance.

After the failed jail break, McCall tried to make a deal with the prosecution and implicate a John Varnes of Deadwood in Wild Bill's murder, in essence claiming that he himself was just a tool not the mastermind behind the shooting. McCall claimed that Varnes paid him to assassinate Wild Bill. McCall also stated that there was another man involved, Tim Brady. The court sent a deputy US marshal to find these two men, but both had vanished. Neither were ever brought to trial or testified in McCall's trail.[10] There was actually some speculation in the press on this question. In an article appearing in the September 8, 1876, St. Paul *Pioneer Press and Tribune*, Leander Richardson, who met Hickok in Deadwood the day before his murder, said that:

> *There were a dozen or more men in Deadwood who wanted to kill Wild Bill because he would not "stand-in" with them on "deadbeat" games [Hickok would not join rigged poker games] but not one man among them all dared to pick a quarrel with him. They were all waiting to get a chance to shoot him in the back . . . The man they charged with the murder [McCall] has a most repulsive visage, and it would require no very keen imagination to picture him as the twin brother of Darwin's Missing Link.[11]*

Was McCall a "patsy," as he claimed to be, or was this just a desperate attempt by a doomed man to escape the noose? History will never know.

McCall's court appearances in Yankton began on December 1 as Judge P. C. Shannon called things to order. At this time McCall received a copy of the indictment against him as well as a list of prosecution witnesses. He was told he had two days to present any motions or pleas. The deputy US marshal also testified that he had been unable to locate McCall's witnesses in Deadwood, and McCall requested that the trial be postponed until April so that his two witnesses could be located, but his motion was denied the next morning in court. Thus McCall's trial began in earnest on December 4 at 10 o'clock in the morning. The local newspaper, the Yankton *Press and Dakotaian* (now known as the *Press and Dakotan*), closely followed the developments of the trial. It described McCall's entrance into court and noted that he had irons on his wrists:

> . . . *which were, however, removed after he had taken his seat within the bar. He manifested no excitement or emotion, though there was a trace of anxiety exhibited in his general demeanor when first brought into court . . . After he had been in court long enough to become accustomed to his new situation he put on a bold front and a careless air, conversing freely with his attorneys and carrying the manner of one who was arraigned for a trifling offense against the law. As the examination of the jury proceeded and the box began to fill with those who were to decide the question of life or death for him, McCall began to exhibit symptoms of nervousness. He scanned closely with his sharp, eager eyes the face of each juror as he took his seat and then anxiously awaited the appearance of the next candidate for examination as to his qualifications to act in the case.*[12]

The jurors were John Treadway, who was elected the foreman; Hiram Dunham; William Box; George Pike; Lewis Clark; West Negus; Charles Edwards; Isaac Esmay; Henry Mowry; Nelson Armstrong; James Withee; and Martin Winchell. One of the observers of all the courtroom action was Wild Bill's brother Lorenzo, who had traveled from Illinois to Yankton for the trial to represent the family's interests.[13] The court adjourned for lunch on December 4 but recommenced at two o'clock, and the prosecution called its first witness, George Shingle, who made the following statement:

*I reside in Cheyenne and have lived there nine months. On the 2nd of August I was at Deadwood in the Black Hills. I knew a man named Wild Bill and had known him since 1866 by that name and by his right name, Hickock [sic]. He was best known by the name of Wild Bill. He is dead. He died in Deadwood on the 2nd day of August, 1876. Deadwood is on Whitewood creek I think. It was at that time a place of 4,000 population, I should think. On the 2nd of August in a saloon at Deadwood kept by Carl Mann and Jerry Lewis, Wild Bill was there playing cards. There was a party of 3 or 4 others sitting at the same table. I was in the room at the time. I saw a man come in the saloon who is here now. It is the defendant here present. He walked towards the back door of the saloon. When within three or four feet of the door he turned and came up behind Wild Bill. He put a pistol within 2 or 3 feet of Wild Bill's head and fired. As he fired he said, "Take that." The ball entered the back part of Wild Bill's head and came out of the right cheek entering the left wrist of Captain Massey [sic]. The shot killed Wild Bill almost instantly. He did not move and said nothing. He sat in the chair a couple of minutes and then fell over backwards. I made an examination of Wild Bill and found him dead. The saloon stood nearly the same as this court house, with a door in each end and a bar and tables inside. The table where Wild Bill sat was nearly in the middle of the room. He was facing the bar.*

*When the defendant came in I was weighing out gold dust . . . After firing the defendant walked backward toward the back door, with his revolver in his hand holding it up. As I went to look at Bill, McCall pointed the revolver at me and snapped it. I got out of the house. Carl Mann was the only one left in the house, and McCall. Saw the defendant half an hour later, when he was arrested. Was present at the trial, which was held in a theater building in Deadwood on the third day of August. McCall said to the court that he had killed Wild Bill and that he was glad of it, and that if he had to do it over he would do the same thing—that Bill had killed a brother of his and he did it for revenge. The weapon used was a Sharps improved revolver 18 inches long with a piece of buckskin sewed around the stock.*[14]

When Shingle was then cross-examined by McCall's defense counsel, he made the following statements:

> *I said I was weighing out gold dust. The room where the bar was was 24 feet wide. The bar took up 8 feet of the room and was 20 feet long. I was standing at the bar. The room was about 80 feet long. Bill was sitting with his back to the back door and fronting the bar. McCall got around alongside of this partition and came up behind Bill. Captain Massie and Wild Bill were having a dispute about the game and I looked up, when I saw McCall in the act of shooting. Wild Bill was prospecting most of the time in the Hills. He did not keep a faro bank. I know of Bill killing three men, but in self defense and was tried and acquitted. He was not a constant drinker. I saw the defendant in Deadwood, but was not acquainted with him. Wild Bill was sober when this shooting occurred. Could not say that McCall was drunk. I do not know that the man was staggering from drunkenness after the shooting. I saw him going up the street with his pistol in his hand, clearing the way, but I don't know he was drunk.*
>
> *The killing occurred about 3 or 4 PM. Eight persons were in the room when the shooting occurred. The affair caused great excitement and a crowd gathered. McCall was acquitted on his trial in Deadwood. There were lawyers and a Judge present and a jury of twelve men. I was there through the whole trial. There was an attorney for the prosecution and defense. I don't know that there were any inducements held out to cause McCall to say that he had killed Wild Bill.*[15]

The next prosecution witness called was Carl Mann, owner of Saloon #10 saloon where Hickok was killed. Mann was a close friend of Hickok's and testified as follows:

> *I reside at Deadwood and was there August 2nd of this year. The place was then a town of two hundred houses. It is on White Wood creek. Gayville is about a mile and a half west of Deadwood Gulch. Crook City is very nearly east of Deadwood—a little north of east. Bear Butte is a little north of east from Crook City. Deadwood may*

*be about eight miles further west than Bear Butte. On the second of last August I had a house in Deadwood. There was a saloon there that some of them said I was keeping. I do not know as I ought to answer questions about my keeping a saloon as it might get me into trouble. There was a building there which I had an interest in and I knew a man named Wild Bill. Saw both him and defendant that day at that building. Know of a shooting affair there that day. It was after dinner, about 3 o'clock probably. Three of us were playing cards with Wild Bill. I heard somebody walking on the floor and as I looked up I saw defendant raise a pistol and fire it at Wild Bill's head. It kind of knocked Bill's head forward and then he fell gradually back. I saw where a bullet came out on his face before he fell. The pistol was from one foot to eighteen inches from Bill's head. It was a navy size revolver [referring to the Colt 1851 model revolver, often called the "Navy"]. The same ball hit Captain Massie in the arm. I slipped off to get something to defend myself with. All went out of my house. McCall pointed his pistol on me and head [sic] it on me all the time. He went out before I did. Do not know of any inducements to defendant to confess. Heard men said that if McCall got up and said Wild Bill killed his brother the jury would clear him. Did not hear anybody say so to McCall. McCall said Wild Bill had killed his brother and he had killed Wild Bill. Did not hear him say anything about doing it again. Saw McCall only twice before this happened and in this house. Bill was there and McCall weighed out some gold dust to get some chips to play poker with Bill and the others. McCall won $23 or $24. Am not certain of the amount. He then went out and came back and played again. After playing a short time he took a purse from his pocket and bet five or six dollars and Bill bet twenty or twenty-five more. McCall shoved his purse further onto the board and says "I call you." Bill won and they came to the bar and asked me to weigh out $20 or $25. The purse was $16.50 short. Bill said "You owe me $16.50." McCall said "Yes" and went out. He came back shortly after and Bill said "Did I break you?" McCall said "Yes." Bill gave him all the change he had, 75 cents, to buy his supper with and told him that if he quit winner in the game he was playing he would* *give him more. McCall would not take the money and went out in fifteen or twenty minutes.*[16]

Mann's sworn testimony affirms Hickok's generosity, and makes the murder even stranger. There seems to have been little reason for McCall to gun Hickok down unless he hated the fact that he was broke and dependent on Wild Bill's largesse for his next meal.[17] It does seem very likely from the testimony offered that McCall's defense that he was avenging a brother that Wild Bill had killed was simply a convenient blind that McCall expected to clear him in an "eye for an eye" frontier environment. It simply did not stand up to examination.

The court resumed action at nine o'clock on December 5 and the prosecution called its next witness, Captain William Massie. Massie was sworn in and testified:

*I reside in St. Louis. Was present in Deadwood at the time of the death of Wild Bill. Was there at the time this man shot him. Did not see him die and do not know that he died immediately. We were seated at a round table playing cards. The house fronted south. I was sitting with my back partly towards the south and partly towards the wall. Bill was seated opposite me at the table. Mr. Mann sat on my right and Charlie at my left. Carl Mann's back was directly towards the front door and Bill's back was towards the back door. I saw the defendant first on that occasion.*

*When the pistol report came I was looking down at the table and looked up and saw the defendant backing as if to get out of the back door. My left arm was resting on the table when the pistol was fired. I felt a shock and numbness in my left wrist. I heard the report of the pistol and looked up to see where it came from and saw the defendant with a pistol in his right hand. He was moving it about apparently to keep the crowd from coming upon him and was backing towards the back door. He was saying, "come on ye s—s of b—s." He intimidated the crowd with the pistol and all got out of the front door except Mr. Mann. I got out quick as I could and did not see Wild Bill fall. I looked up at the pistol and my eyes passed him. The ball was not found*

*on examining my arm. It is there yet I suppose. I saw the defendant*
*come into the same room a day or two before and around behind Bill*
*and pull his pistol about two thirds out. There was a young man with*
*him who put his arm around the defendant and walked him towards*
*the back door.*[18]

One has to wonder why in the world didn't Massie alert Wild Bill
to McCall if he had partially pulled a pistol out near Wild Bill the day
before. After Massie's testimony, however, the prosecution swiftly finished up their case. They called Joseph Mitchell who testified:

*I reside at this time in Sioux City [Iowa], but in the early part of*
*August in this year was in Deadwood. At the time Wild Bill was*
*killed I was putting the wainscoting in the same room. Saw the*
*defendant there after the shooting but did not notice him before. The*
*report of a revolver was the first that attracted my attention. I next*
*noticed Wild Bill lying on the floor. McCall was standing by the back*
*door. He pointed his revolver at me and told me to . . . come on. I then*
*went out of the door at the rear of the building.*[19]

Although McCall's defense counselors, General Beadle and Oliver
Shannon, had no witnesses, they also focused on the details, making a
motion to discharge McCall by claiming that the prosecution had failed
to deliver an accurate copy of the indictment—an obvious attempt to stall
the proceedings. An argument ensued, and the court ordered the defense
to produce the copy of the indictment they had received the next morning. The next day Oliver Shannon addressed the court, and his remarks
were recorded as follows:

*Mr. Shannon further says, in handing the paper to the court, that the*
*Indictment was read to the defendant in open court, and this paper, or*
*alleged copy of the Indictment, was handed to him after the prisoner*
*had that day been remanded. Mr. Shannon again admits that it was on*
*the day of the arraignment, that he received this paper. U.S. Atty., Mr.*
*Pound then presents his affidavit to the Court, as to the service of said*

*paper on Mr. Shannon in the presence of the said prisoner, on the 18th of October A.D. 1876, the day of the arraignment, which affidavit is written on the back of said paper—and the Court having endorsed the said paper, identifying . . . the said paper with all its said endorsements is now ordered to be filed and to be . . . of record in this case.*[20]

The judge presiding over the trial, P. C. Shannon, presented his opinion on the issue of the indictment or lack thereof:

*A true copy of the Indictment in the present case was delivered to the counsel of defendant (and in his presence, as positively sworn to by the U.S. Attorney) 47 days before the trial; secondly, a defective copy was delivered to the defendant himself, 3 days before the trial; thirdly, the plea of the 18th of October, could have been withdrawn, during the interval, for any advantageous purpose, but no attempt to do so was made—the defendant and his counsel thereby tacitly acquiescing (after abundant time for deliberation) in the propriety and wisdom of the original plea; and lastly, the defendant, without making any objection, went to the jury on that case. By having entered upon trial, and by having waited until the prosecution closed its case, the defendant was too late to make the objections referred to, concerning those copies; for, by such conduct and acquiescence, he has virtually admitted that he had a copy sufficient for all purposes intended by the act of congress. As to the objection that the defendant should have been indicted and tried on the other side of this court, it is well settled that a trial for homicide, committed in an Indian reserve, must be had on the Federal side of a Territorial court, and is governed by U.S. Statutes and the rules of the common law . . . It is therefore considered and adjudged that the motions for a new trial, and in arrest of judgement be, and they are hereby overruled.*[21]

The case was referred to the jury at seven o'clock in the evening on December 6, and they were "charged by the court, and retired in the charge of Henry C. Ash and F. D. Wysman, deputies of the U.S. Marshal, and the bailiffs of this Court, who were first duly and legally sworn to keep the said jury together in some private and convenient place, without food and drink, except bread and water unless otherwise ordered by the Court, and not to permit any person to speak or communicate with them, or ask them whether they have agreed upon the verdict, and to return them into Court when they have so agreed, or when ordered by the Court."[22] (The order for the jury to be denied food and drink except for bread and water appears to have been a result of members of the jury visiting a saloon and buying liquor.[23])

The jury deliberated for only three hours, returning to the court at ten fifteen that same evening. When they were asked for their verdict, which was handed to the court by the foreman of the jury, John Treadway, it read, "Guilty as charged in the Indictment." McCall was escorted from the courtroom by the marshal, while Wild Bill's brother Lorenzo expressed his satisfaction with the outcome and commented to the local newspaper that "there was no truth in the assertion that Wild Bill shot the brother of McCall in Kansas."[24]

It must have been a great relief to Lorenzo and the entire Hickok family that Wild Bill's murderer would finally pay for the cold-blooded murder of their brother, son, and friend.

When the court reconvened on January 3 for McCall's sentencing, McCall addressed the court and basically pled for his life, but to no avail. Judge Shannon handed down the following sentence:

> *Whereupon all the singular and the premises being seen, and by the said Court here fully understood, it is considered by the Court here, and the judgement of the law being so the sentence of the Court is, that you, John McCall, alias Jack McCall, be remanded hence to the place whence you came, that you be then imprisoned until Thursday the first day of March, A.D. 1877, upon which day you shall be thence conducted to the place of execution, where, between the hours of 9 o'clock in the forenoon and 2 o'clock in the afternoon of the said day, you shall be hanged by the neck until you shall be dead. (And may the Lord have mercy on your soul).*[25]

McCall's attorneys filed a motion for a new trial and attempted to negate the verdict by finding inaccuracies in the written judgment, but their efforts proved unsuccessful. Their greatest attempt to clear their client was soon to come, however, in the form of a petition to the president of the United States (Ulysses S. Grant) for commutation of his sentence to life imprisonment instead of death by hanging. On the same day as McCall's sentencing, McCall's attorneys informed the prosecution and Judge Shannon that they had filed the proper paperwork for a pardon or a commutation of their client's sentence.[26] McCall's attorneys cited various items in their petition to the president, including the apparent lack of a motive in the case (apparently rejecting their client's own earlier assertions that it was a revenge killing for McCall's brother supposedly killed by Wild Bill) and alleging that the extenuating circumstance of alcohol consumption played into their client's actions. The governor of Dakota Territory, John Pennington, also wrote part of the petition arguing for McCall's pardon, noting:

*The prisoner's statement to the Court, impressed the truthfulness of it on nearly all when he gave the circumstances of the debauch that preceded the homicide. His statement was that the first he knew of the killing was whilst sitting on a log in the outskirts of the village with five or six men around him and when returning to consciousness was told that he "had got into a bad scrape" and when asked what it was, was told by them that he had killed "Wild Bill."[27] Your petitioners further would most respectfully that last August when the homicide occurred, was a very early period in the history of the Black Hills, when pioneers, marauders, gamblers and all sorts of people common to new countries, were there, and all thus really in violation of law, and every man taking his chances—"Wild Bill," a notorious character among them. Whilst this, of course, is no excuse for crime, they are circumstances that always beget a sad state of morals and an atmosphere around, for which no one individual is responsible, and which by accident, puts him in positions for which he is no more responsible. In view, therefore, of all the facts, we as citizens of Dakota Territory, desiring law and order and punishment of crime, think it prudent and right to ask for executive clemency in this case, which will bring the penalty short of the death penalty.*[28]

It is certainly alarming to read a territorial governor arguing for the mitigation of a murder because, basically, "everybody is doing it."

Along with the governor's petition, McCall's attorneys also submitted one that was signed by various local dignitaries including the speaker of the House of Representatives. In their petition, the attorneys gave their reasoning why they believed McCall qualified for a pardon:

*1. Having more intimate relations with the prisoner as his Counsel, we have on our honor and under our oaths the most serious doubts of the guilt of the accused. That he killed the deceased we have no doubt but that he murdered him we do not believe.*

*2. In the closest professional communication with the prisoner, he has never been able (or if able has utterly failed to do so) to tell us of an act or incident connected with the killing or to assign a motive for it.*

*3. All of the facts as detailed by the evidence fail to show any object of revenge—any hatred or ill-will. Both parties had been drinking and gambling together; but no quarrel had ensued.*[29] *The time and place & circumstances forbid any natural conclusion that money was the motive. The acts of the accused immediately after the shooting, admit readily, in our judgement, of the conclusion that he was either crazy drunk or had symptoms of delirium tremens.*

*4. The prisoner was perhaps unfortunate in having no money and of course had few friends. The Court on his petition allowed him a subpoena for two witnesses but no more. They could not be found by the time the deputy Marshal got back to the Black Hills, having gone as we were informed into a new section of the country over which there was an excitement at the time of the new gold discoveries. By these two witnesses particularly we expected to prove the debauch of the prisoner before and at about the time of the homicide. Being without a witness he was of course without the means of putting in a palliating circumstance from his side of the case.*

*5. We have no word to utter about the deceased. We knew him only from reputation as "Wild Bill" and propose that the grass that grows over his grave may be as green and beautiful as that of any other spot; but all the surroundings call to mind an important consideration in this case for the mind of the executive that could not be entertained under the rigid rules of evidence by the Court and jury, viz: It was a place where there was no law, no order, no society, no refinement, no church, no school, no home for the wayward and erring, no one to give advice or wholesome counsel, no friend to take the youthful arm and take him aside when he would rush into the haunts of saloon hells for the fiery whiskey that mad men made [sic], reeled their intellect and dethroned their reason. At such a moment, at such a time, in such a place we find this youthful prisoner of 24 author of a homicide!*

*For these reasons and others that might be urged—without any appeal to feeling of sympathy; but to the mature judgment in the just appreciation of all surroundings, and remembering that "mercy shall rejoice against judgment" we ask for the exercise of executive clemency, at least commuting the sentence.*[30]

This so-called "environmental" defense is quite common today—excuse a criminal's conduct because he was beaten as a child, because he was raised by an alcoholic, because he was taught no moral values, and so on. It may have been rather novel, however, in 1876! After the petitions for clemency arrived at the Department of Justice in Washington, they were communicated in turn to US Attorney William Pound, asking him to contact the trial judge and render a complete report on the matter. Pound proceeded with his task, delivering his report on February 7. His long reply is worth quoting as it casts new insight into the character of McCall and Hickok:[31]

*Sir,*

*I am in receipt of your letter of the 1st instant, with inclosures (sic) (which are herewith returned) relative to the commutation of the sentence of death in the case of John McCall, alias Jack McCall. As* directed in your letter, I have communicated, verbally, with Chief Justice Shannon, who presided at the trial, with a view to obtaining such an expression of his opinion in the matter as he might be disposed to make, but he stated that he felt a delicacy about interfering in any way; which I believe being his invariable course upon such occasions. The petition, although not numerously signed, contains the names of the Governor and two other Territorial officers, who were actuated as I learn, almost entirely by their dislike for capital punishment, and not by a knowledge of any extenuating circumstances in this case. None of them heard the testimony, or attended the trial so as to obtain a knowledge of the facts as detailed by witnesses. No single person who did hear the testimony, whether as a juror, officer of the Court or spectator is found to join in the request [for pardon]. A majority of the grand and petit jury panels live in this place, or within two or three miles of it, and this is true of eight of the petit jurors who tried McCall, notwithstanding the statement of Mr. Shannon in his letter that a number of them "live 40 to 60 miles away over the prairie country." I have never known a case where the interests of a prisoner were more carefully guarded by the Court than this one. Witnesses were sent for at the expense of the Government, where there were grave doubts as to their materiality, and the trial postponed nearly two months, and it was only after the Marshal made his return, and it was evident that no such witnesses as he desired could be obtained, and the trial proceeded. The prisoner was given the benefit of all doubtful questions raised during the trial, and upon taking the case to the Supreme Court of the Territory, the judgement of the District Court was unanimously affirmed by a full bench. Upon the question of drunkenness, which is urged in this petition as a main reason for the commutation of his sentence, the Court in its charge to the jury declared it their right and duty, if they had, from all the evidence, a reasonable doubt that the prisoner acted with a mind so clear and unclouded as to be able to form and execute a deliberate purpose, to convict of manslaughter only. So favorable, indeed, to the prisoner was the charge, throughout, that no exception was taken to it. The murder having been a deliberate assassination, of the most cowardly *character, an effort seems to be made now again, as it was on the trial, to excuse or palliate the act by a reference to the peculiar condition of society as then existed in the Black Hills. In the same connection, while conceding that this is scarcely an excuse for assassinating him, counsel find it convenient to refer to the deceased as a "notorious character" and as one whose real name was only disclosed by the evidence. A reference to the indictment will show that both his real name and the alias of "Wild Bill" were used in it. But the name "Wild Bill" had been given to him and fastened upon him so that he was really better known by that than by any other, and without any discredit to himself. It is a part of the history of the war, that this man, by reason of his fearless and efficient service as a Union scout among the guerillas of Missouri, Arkansas and Eastern Kansas, and by his contests with these same guerillas even after the war closed, when they so persistently pursued him, won by this name of "Wild Bill," and he certainly had no reason during his life to be ashamed of it. The same policy pursued him even to the Black Hills, his old enemies giving him a bad name whenever and wherever they dared to do it. Although the evidence was clearly inadmissible in a case like this, where the prisoner sought the deceased, and while in no danger, shot him from behind, I did not object to, and the court permitted testimony as to the character of the deceased for violence. One witness, for some years a passenger conductor on the Kansas Pacific Railway, who knew him there, ten years or more ago, and who had known him since at Cheyenne and in the Black Hills, said he was not a quarrelsome man and never quarreled unless forced into it. Other witnesses gave him the same character and no one gave him a different one. How many aliases the prisoner has, it would be difficult to tell. Although declaring upon his arraignment that his true name was John McCall, he asserted immediately before sentence was passed upon him that it was not his true name. **He seems to be a person of a depraved and wicked heart**[32] [author's emphasis] as was shown by a murderous attack upon the keeper of the jail here, in an attempt to escape, a short time before his trial. Coming, as it is now asserted from the South, he had conceived for some cause, or without a* cause, an especial hatred for "Wild Bill."[33] The testimony shows that some days before the homicide, McCall had pushed himself into a game of cards with "Wild Bill." He bet more than he had and lost his money. Wild Bill told him he could pay when he was able to, and offered to lend him some money for his immediate wants. Although the offer seemed to be made in the most kindly spirit, McCall became angry, rejected the money and left the house. The next day, while Wild Bill was again seated at a table, playing cards, McCall was seen to come up behind him, with his eyes on him, put his hand back on his revolver, and draw it about half way out, when another man, not known to the witness, took McCall by the arm and led him away. A day or two later at a time when "Wild Bill" was again seated at a table, quietly playing cards with three other men, McCall came in, passed towards the back part of the room, came to a point directly behind Wild Bill, drew his revolver, held it within two feet of the back of his head, and while his victim was evidently entirely unconscious of his presence, sent a bullet entirely through his head. McCall instantly turned his revolver upon the others present, swinging the muzzle with the utmost steadiness from one to the another, thereby clearing the room.[34] He then passed out at the door in the same way, keeping his revolver turned towards those nearest to him, passed rapidly to where a horse was tied which he attempted to mount. The saddle turned and he started up the street, clearing the way as he went, and was finally captured about an hour and a half afterward. These facts were proven by four creditable witnesses who were carefully questioned in regard to McCall's intoxication. They stated that while he might have been drinking some, and probably had been, he showed no signs of intoxication, and did not stagger or stumble and showed the utmost coolness and deliberation in every movement. I certainly do not seek the life of this unfortunate man, and if I should consult my own feelings and inclinations, I should prefer a substitution for life to the death penalty as a punishment for murder. The law of the United States recognizes the latter, however, and not the former, and upon my conscience I am utterly unable to see any extenuating *circumstances in this case. The murder was deliberately planned, and executed in a cruel and cowardly manner, by a man who evidently has no regard whatever for human life. If the death penalty is to be inflicted in any case, I do not see upon what real ground the proposed leniency would be based in this particular case. As a legal proposition, can this sentence be safely commuted to imprisonment for life? The United States law recognizes but two grades of homicide and two degrees of punishment. There is no intermediate ground between ten years of imprisonment for manslaughter and the death penalty for murder. It is true that the President can grant a conditional pardon, but the prisoner being in close custody may neither accept or reject this condition. He is carried away in irons, and the time for his execution passes:- may he not then claim that he has neither accepted nor rejected the commutation proposed, which is a change to a sentence not recognized in law?*

*Very Respectfully, Your Obedient Servant,*
*Wm. Pound, U.S. Attorney*[35]

While McCall's petitions were considered in Washington, Marshal Burdick, back in Yankton, was anxious to know the results of McCall's attorney's efforts, as it was his duty to prepare the scaffold if McCall was to be hanged. He wrote a letter to Washington, DC, asking for notification if McCall was to be spared:

*Dear Judge,*

*I wish you would do me the favor to call at the office of the Attorney General at as early an hour as will suit your convenience after the receipt of this, and learn if you can whether McCall's sentence will be commuted by the President or not. Should you learn that it will be, please suggest to the Attorney General the propriety of his telegraphing me to that effect, as I must commence preparations as soon as one week from tomorrow, and don't want to incur any expenses to the Government unless there is a necessity for it. It really seems to me that he ought to advise me by telegraph that the sentence will be commuted or that it will not be, as the case may be, that I may have time to make the necessary preparations, or that none need be made.*

*Respectfully,*
*J. H. Burdick*[36]

Burdick's concerns were alleviated with the receipt of the following telegram from Washington on February 19:

*Department of Justice, To J. H. Burdick, U.S. Marshal, Yankton, Dakota Territory: The Attorney General directs me to say to you that he has considered the application made on behalf of John McCall, convicted of murder, and declines to interfere with the sentence pronounced by the Court, A. R. Dutton, Chief Clerk.*[37]

According to witnesses and newspaper information, McCall remained fairly emotionless during his last days on Earth. He began regularly reading the Bible and frequently spoke with a Catholic priest, Father Daxacher. He also wrote several letters to various people who had written him in prison. He wrote one to the editor at the *Press and Dakotaian* as follows:

*Editor, Sir:*

*I intend to write an article which I wish you to publish in your paper after my death. If you will be here the day the execution takes place, I will hand it to you. If you accept or decline please let me know.*

*John McCall*[38]

The contents of this article have forever remained a mystery because McCall apparently changed his mind and ripped up the letter the night before he was hanged.[39]

While he was awaiting the completion of his sentence, Marshal Burdick received a letter that he duly passed on to McCall:

*To the Marshal of Yankton,*
*Dear Sir,*

*I saw in the morning papers a piece about the sentence of the murderer of Wild Bill, Jack McCall. There was a young man of the name of John McCall left here about six years ago, who has not been heard from for the last three years. He has a father, mother, and three sisters living here in Louisville, who were very uneasy about him since they heard about the murder of Wild Bill. If you can send us any information about him, we would be very thankful to you. This John McCall is about twenty-five years old, has light hair, inclined to curl, and one eye crossed. I cannot say about his height, as he was not grown when he left here. Please write as soon as convenient, as we are anxious to hear from you.*

*Very Respectfully,*
*Mary A. McCall.*[40]

No one knows whether the author of the letter was a relative of Jack McCall or if McCall had family in Louisville. Much of Jack McCall's history and the true motives for his actions will forever remain a mystery, in the realm of speculative hypothesis.

McCall's day of judgment arrived on March 1, 1877. He was visited by the Catholic priest Daxacher before he left the jail for the gallows. Marshal Burdick came to McCall's cell at nine o'clock in the morning and read him the death warrant. He left his cell at nine thirty with the marshal and his assistants. They were transported to the scaffold in several carriages, one for the marshal and one for McCall and newspaper men. According to the reporters, McCall said nothing on the two-mile trip to the gallows. He was led up the scaffold by a Deputy Ash who placed the black cap over his head and put the noose around his neck. McCall, who was grasping a crucifix in his hands, said, "Draw it tighter Marshal."

The door of the gallows opened at ten fifteen, and Jack McCall, mystery murderer of Wild Bill Hickok, swung into eternity. McCall's last words were reported to be, "Oh God!" as he fell. He was cut down from the rope twelve minutes later and examined by doctors D. F. Etter and J. M. Miller, who noted that even in death he still grasped his crucifix. He was laid in a walnut coffin and buried in the southwest corner of the Catholic cemetery, remaining there until the cemetery was removed in 1881.[41]

# Epilogue: The Myth of Wild Bill

By the time of his death at the hand of Jack McCall, Wild Bill Hickok was a legend throughout the United States, if not the world, for his legendary prowess in a gunfight and for his storied appearances with Buffalo Bill. However, one of his early biographers noted that shortly before his death, Hickok, "remained inactive owing to an attack of ophthalmia superinduced no doubt from the exposure he underwent while in the Black Hills. Dr. Thorne treated him for several months with such success that his eyesight, which was for a time entirely destroyed, was partly restored, but he never again regained his perfect vision."[1]

Author Mari Sandoz asserted that his condition was advanced glaucoma—a disease that soon would have caused complete blindness in the famed sharpshooter. She wrote that Hickok had been examined by an army doctor at Camp Carlin in Wyoming, a fact asserted by other writers as well. Despite heroic efforts by historian Joseph Rosa to obtain government records of this medical visit, however, no documents have ever been uncovered in any military or civilian archives substantiating this episode. That said, Sandoz wrote that by the time of his death Hickok knew the danger he was in, saying, "There's a hundred as would brace me on any street, if it gets out how little I can see—the doctor promised to do what he could, but it would be little."[2] The sharpshooter's career was likely coming to an end one way or another.

After Wild Bill's death, his wife, Agnes, went on to marry again and to tour as an entertainer with her daughter, Emma. Both Emma and Agnes had stellar reputations as performers, even without their connection to Wild Bill, but their connection to the famous gunfighter and lawman followed them for the rest of their recorded lives. Emma was identified in the press as "the daughter of Wild Bill's widow. Mrs. Agnes Lake Hickok accompanies her daughter everywhere and is her constant companion. She has herself had 36 years of experience with circuses and what she don't know about them is not worth thinking about."[3]

There is also an interesting story about an unknown son/stepson of Agnes and Wild Bill that appeared in the Sioux City *Journal*, and was also reprinted in the Cheyenne *Daily Leader*. The Sioux City *Journal*, of the first instance, says:

> *A son of Wild Bill, the well-known frontier character who was killed by Jack McCall, at Deadwood, is in the city [Sioux City, Iowa] on his way to join an uncle in the Black Hills. His mother was accidentally killed at Denver not long since, by a shot fired by a drunken man at somebody else. The young man himself is lame from a bullet lodged in his leg by a brother of his father's murderer, with whom he had an altercation. His step mother, Madam Lake, once lived at Cheyenne. She took charge of her husband's circus after his death, and while traveling with it was married to Wild Bill. It will be seen that a pay streak of tragedy runs through the whole family.*[4]

This gentleman, whether fictional or true, was never heard of again, nor was he ever located by subsequent Wild Bill researchers. It was probably a fabrication designed to sell newspapers—not an unknown in the case of Wild Bill.

And Wild Bill's reputation followed him into his grave. A macabre follow-up to the burial and internment of Wild Bill's body occurred several years after his death, when it was decided to reinter his body, and many others, in a new cemetery called Mount Moriah near Deadwood. In September 1879, Colorado Charlie, Lewis Schoenfield, and John McClintock decided to remove Wild Bill's body from his first grave and rebury him in the new grave. Immediately after his death, there were conflicting stories about the condition of his body. Some said that they had seen knife and bullet wounds on his body prior to burial, but this is contradicted by an Ellis Pierce, a barber who assisted with the burial, who said that Hickok was not undressed at all before he was buried.

However, when it was moved and reinterred at Mount Moriah, Hickok's body was removed from its original coffin and his body was visible, which McClintock reported on:

*Here the box was opened and the lid of the casket was removed. The body down to the hips was exposed. To our great astonishment, it appeared to be in a perfect state of preservation. Being perfectly white, it seemed to have a coat of lime finish. The clothes, which were decomposed, had evidently been jolted to the sides while in transit to the new grave, leaving the upper portion of the body exposed. The manifold pleats in the fine linen shirt which he wore showed plainly on his form. The writer [McClintock] took a stick the size of a cane and tapped many places on the body, face, and head, discovering no soft places anywhere. While the body appeared to be solid, petrified, the sound from the tapping was much the same as would result from the tapping of a wall, and not of solid stone. Some of the party were inclined to believe that the body was in a process of petrification . . . While it was an extremely heavy load for four able-bodied men to carry up the hill, the writer would not place the weight above 400 pounds, nor did I concur in the belief that it was a case of petrification, though there may have been such cases in existence. It was my belief that it was the result of a natural embalming by percolation of water containing embalming substances, depositing these in the tissues of the body. After a close examination had been made by the four of us, the lid of the coffin was fastened down and the body of the great gunman, one of the greatest man-killers that the world has ever known, was for a second time lowered into a grave to be covered and lost to view. The wooded headboard was moved to the new grave, where it was practically destroyed by relic hunters whittling off pieces. In 1891, a statue was erected by J. B. Riordan, a sculptor from New York who chanced to be in Deadwood. This consisted of a rock pedestal with inscription, including the name of the sculptor, surmounted by a bust of Wild Bill. This was badly mutilated by relic hunters and in 1902 another monument was placed over the grave. This is a life-sized Black Hills sandstone figure of Wild Bill. It was sculptured by Alvin Smith in a shop owned by H. W. Guyor, in Deadwood, and was erected in 1903. It is also badly defaced by relic hunters and the weather. It was tightly enclosed for protection with a heavy wire screen, but this was cut open by relic hunters, so it was removed about twenty years ago.*[5]

One of truly remarkable results of the story of Wild Bill Hickok is its enduring popularity. Even today, well over 140 years after his death, Hickok is frequently mentioned in Western magazines, movies, and novels. He seems to be generally regarded as the greatest and the most dangerous gunmen from the Old West.

# Appendix: Guns and Techniques of a Legend

Wild Bill Hickok was famous for his gunfights, and he in turn made several guns famous. Perhaps the most well-known pistol Hickok used was the Colt Model 1851 "Navy" pistol. The Colt has an interesting history even without its association with Wild Bill.

Samuel Colt, the father of the American handgun, obtained a patent for his multishot revolving pistol revolver, which became known as the Colt Paterson revolver, from the British government in 1835 and received similar patents from the United States in 1836. Although primitive by modern standards, it was a sea change in gun manufacturing for the world. Colt had managed to develop a six-shot revolving cylinder pistol that was both fairly reliable and easily mass-produced. The gun became a favorite of the Texas Rangers, who famously engaged a Comanche Indian force led by Chief Yellow Wolf with their new weapons. The Colt Paterson proved to be a game-changer for the Rangers, particularly as it now became possible for mounted men to fire their pistols several times without stopping and reloading. Although the Paterson proved successful, Colt suffered financial reverses and closed his factory in 1843. His fortunes revived when a young Texas Ranger named Samuel Walker befriended Colt. Together they developed a new and even more fearsome pistol, the Colt Walker (or the Walker Colt if you prefer). The advent of the Mexican-American War and the Rangers' use of the new gun granted Colt publicity and sales.[1]

Hickok's favorite pistol, the 1851 Colt Navy, was the next logical progression in the development of Sam Colt's firearms empire. The 1851 Colt became known simply as the "Navy" possibly because the caliber (.36) was specified by the Department of the Navy.[2] Others have suggested that the name comes from a small engraving on the cylinder of the pistol. The engraving shows a battle between ships of the Texas "navy" and Mexican ships, and is dated May 16, 1843.[3] Whichever story you choose to believe, this was the primary weapon employed by Hickok in most of his gunfights. Hickok usually carried two of them and wore them butts-forward in his belt or in a sash. He began with standard walnut-handled pistols, but later switched to more showy ivory-handled guns.[4] The guns were long and somewhat cumbersome, so the standard method of drawing these firearms was not the quick snap and grab that we see in Western movies, but rather a technique known as the Reverse or Plains draw, which had the pistoleer reach down for the guns (which were carried butts-forward), grab the handles, and pull out the pistols while turning them around and facing them toward their target. This obviously took some practice, but Hickok was always the fastest and most accurate draw in any exchange of lead. Hickok's familiarity with his weapon of choice was certainly a major factor in his survival, as noted in the following observation on his preparedness for a possible gun battle:

> . . . to my surprise as soon as Bill was dressed, all but coat and hat—he went carefully to the door and looked all around for several moments then emptied one 6 shooter. He had the one in each hand, returned to the room, cleaned and reloaded it, then went to the door and emptied the other one and reloaded it the same way. Bill used powder and ball—we had pistols then with metal cartridges but Bill would not use them. He used powder and ball, moulded his own bullets and primed each tube using a pin to push the powder in so he was sure of powder contact and before putting on the cap he looked at the interior of each cap. Now this was all strange to me and new too, for I had roomed and slept with Bill all the time he was at the drover's cottage and he never did it there so I said, did you get your guns damp yesterday Bill? He said "no, but I ain't ready to go yet and I am not taking any chances, when I draw and pull I must be sure."[5]

His preparation was important, but so were his cold-as-ice nerves. Many people can shoot accurately at a stationary target, and a few can probably even shoot at a person with ease and accuracy, but it is a rare individual who has the focus to aim carefully and fire at an enemy who is armed and firing back at you. This was Hickok's notable distinction. As the Chicago *Tribune* noted in 1876:

> *The secret of Bill's success was his ability to draw and discharge his pistols, with a rapidity that was truly wonderful, and a peculiarity of his was that the two were presented and discharged simultaneously, being "out and off" before the average man had time to think about it. He never seemed to take any aim, yet he never missed. Bill never did things by halves. When he drew his pistols it was always to shoot, and it was a theory of his that every man did the same.*[6]

Hickok's friend and famed frontiersman Buffalo Bill Cody made several observations on Wild Bill's pistol skills:

> *Bill beat them to it. He made up his mind to kill the other man before the other man had finished thinking, and so Bill would just quietly pull his gun and give it to him. That was all there was to it. It is easy enough to beat the other man if you start first. Bill always shot as he raised his gun. That is, he was never in a hurry about it; he just pulled the gun from his hip and let it go as he was raising it; shoot on the up-raise, you might call it. Most men lifted the gun higher, then drew it down to cock it before firing. Bill cocked it with his thumb, I guess, as it was coming into line with his man . . . But he was not the quickest man by any means. He was just cool and quiet, and started first. Bill was not a bad man, as is often pictured. But he was a bad man to tackle. Always cool, kind and cheerful, almost about it. And he never killed a man unless that man was trying to kill him. That's fair.*[7]

Cody also commented on the number of shootings his friend participated in and tried to explain why and how Wild Bill survived:

> *He was a man with a whole world of nerve and one of the kindest, best hearted fellows on earth. He seemed to be unfortunate in getting*

*into scrapes, but he always "got" his man when he went for him. He was not actually responsible for many of his battles, but having killed a few men and acquired a considerable degree of notoriety as a quick man with his pistol and a dead shot, he was sought for and compelled to fight. The country was full of bad men, murderous ruffians, who committed reckless deeds, simply for the reputation it gave them. These fellows used to hunt Bill up every time he came into a place and they generally found him when they looked for him. In all the fights he had no one ever succeeded in getting him down. His fatal coolness and his certain aim saved him. The other fellow was quietly buried, for none of Bill's subjects ever went away and got cured so they could make him future trouble.*[8]

# NOTES

## PREFACE: THE GREATEST OF THE GUNMEN

1. George Armstrong Custer, *My Life on the Plains*, Sheldon and Co., New York, 1874, pp. 44–45, originally appearing in *Galaxy* magazine in installments in 1872–1873.

## INTRODUCTION

1. Time-Life Books–The Old West, *The Cowboys*, Time-Life Books, New York, 1973, p. 193; quoting from Joseph McCoy, *Historic Sketches of the Cattle Trade of the West and Southwest*, Kansas City, MO, 1874, reprint, University Nebraska Press, 1986.

2. Joseph Rosa, *Wild Bill Hickock, Gunfighter*, University Oklahoma Press, Norman, 2001, p. 138.

3. Ibid., p. 197.

4. *The Cowboys*, p. 197.

5. Ibid., p. 196.

6. Ibid., p. 193.

7. Ibid., p. 197.

8. Theodore Roosevelt, *Ranch Life and the Hunting Trail*, Century, New York, 1901, p. 114.

9. Leander P. Richardson, "A Trip to the Black Hills," *Scribner's Monthly*, Volume XIII, February 1877, p. 755. My thanks to the USD ID Weeks archivists for helping me locate this old original article.

10. Rosa, *Gunfighter*, pp. 142–143.

## CHAPTER 1: THE BEGINNINGS

1. John McClintock, *Pioneer Days in the Black Hills*, published by the author, Deadwood, South Dakota, 1939, p. 282; J. W. Buel, *Heroes of the Plains*, Standard Publishing Co., Philadelphia, 1886, p. 21.

2. Buel, ibid.

3. *Fremont's First Impressions*, Introduction by Anne Hyde, University Nebraska Press-Lincoln, 2012, p. xvii.

4. Ibid., p. 24.

5. Ibid., p. 24.

6. Ibid.

7. Ibid., p. 367.

8. Ibid.

9. Ibid.

10. Ibid., p. 368.

11. David Kennedy, *The American Pageant* (eleventh edition), Houghton Mifflin Co., Boston, 1998, p. 362.

12. Ibid., p. 364.

13. Ibid., p. 366.

14. Ibid., p. 367.

15. *Selections from Lincoln-Inaugurals, Addresses and Letters*, Longman, Green and Co., New York, 1910, pp. 88–89.

## CHAPTER 2: BLEEDING KANSAS

1. Buel, pp. 27–28.

2. Kennedy, pp. 415, 422.

3. Buel, p. 28.

4. Richardson, p. 2.

5. Hickok triumphed in several such situations when the lead was literally flying in his direction. This, in itself, is remarkable. On one occasion in 1872, Hickok was attending the state fair in Kansas City, Missouri, during a confrontation with fifty Texas cowboys who had ordered a band to play the Southern theme song, *Dixie*. Hickok commanded the bandmaster to cease and desist, and he himself was not injured.

6. W. E. Webb, *Buffalo Land*, E. Hannaford and Co., Chicago, 1872, p. 438.

7. Ibid., p. 447.

8. Buel, p. 29; *Kansas State Historical Society Collections*, Vol. V (1891–1896).

9. Buel, p. 29.

10. Buel, p. 30.

## CHAPTER 3: OVERLAND

1. Mark Twain, *Roughing It*, 1872, quoted in *Wild West*, "When the Stagecoaches Rolled West" by Gregory Lalire, April 2002, p. 48.

2. Buel, p. 30.

3. Buel, p. 30.

4. Joseph Rosa, *They Called Him Wild Bill*, University of Oklahoma Press, Norman, 1964, p. 12.

5. Buel, p. 36.

6. Buel, p. 37; Rosa, *They Called Him Wild Bill*, p. 12.

7. Buel, pp. 37–38.

8. Buel, pp. 40–41.

## CHAPTER 4: THE MAKING OF A LEGEND— THE McCANLESS AFFAIR

1. Allison Hardy, *Wild Bill Hickok-King of the Gunfighters*, Haldeman-Julius Publications, Girard, KS, 1943, pp. 4–5. This book is really a pamphlet-size publication.

2. Colonel G. W. Nichols, "Wild Bill," *Harper's New Monthly Magazine*, February 1867. Again, my thanks to the archivists at ID Weeks Library at the University of South Dakota for locating an original copy of this article.

3. Hardy, p. 5.

4. William Connelly, "Wild Bill–James Butler Hickok," *Kansas State Historical Collections Vol. XVII*, Kansas State Printing, Topeka, 1928, p. 1.

5. Ibid., pp. 4–5.

6. "Testimonial of Monroe McCanless," *Forest and Stream*, December, 1927. I located this in Hardy, p. 6.

7. Ibid.

8. Frank Wilstach quoted in Dawson.

9. Ibid.

## CHAPTER 5: FIRST SHOTS

1. Hardy, p. 8.

2. Ibid.

3. Hardy, p. 9; Nichols, p. 280.

4. *Springfield Patriot*, January 31, 1867, quoted in *Kansas Historical Quarterly*, Vol. 26, 1960, p. 415.

5. Buel, p. 91; Nichols, pp. 276–277.

6. Buel, p. 93; Rosa, *Gunfighter*, p. 55; Hardy, p. 11; Nichols, p. 276.

7. Roosevelt, pp. 13–14.

8. Eyewitness statements made before Greene County Coroner, Greene County Archive, Springfield; quoted in Rosa, *Gunfighter*, pp. 86–90.

9. Greene County Coronor's report, see Rosa, *Gunfighter*, p. 93.

10. Major Albert Barnitz, diary and journals covering the period 1861–1870, Bernitz Papers, the Beinecke Library, Yale University; quoted in Rosa, *Gunfighter*, p. 92.

11. Nichols, p. 277. Note that I have cleaned up Nichols's description of Hickok's grammar. Apparently Nichols thought Hickok's remarks would be more believable if he spoke in a bumpkin-like fashion. There are no written records that indicate Hickok was ever anything but a well-spoken person—in other words, he employed good grammar.

12. July 27 issue of Missouri *Weekly Patriot*; quoted in Rosa, *Gunfighter*, p. 94; quoted in full in *Kansas Historical Society Collections*, Vol. 26, 1960, p. 411.

13. Ibid.

14. Missouri *Weekly Patriot*, August 10, 1865.

## Chapter 6: From Gambler to Marshal

1. Rosa, *Gunfighter*, p. 65.
2. Some of his official actions are listed in the Topeka *Weekly Leader*, April 2, 1868; quoted in Rosa, *Gunfighter*, p. 65.
3. Ibid., p. 66.
4. Rosa, *Gunfighter*, p. 76.
5. Hardy, p. 14.
6. Hardy, p. 14.
7. Ibid., p. 15; Rosa, *Gunfighter*, p. 97.
8. Blaine Burkey, *Wild Bill Hickok–The Law in Hays City*, Ellis County Historical Society, 1973, p. 5.
9. Topeka *Weekly Leader*, April 2, 1868.
10. Ibid., April 13, 1868.
11. Rosa, *Gunfighter*, p. 99.
12. Hardy, p. 15.
13. Rosa, *Gunfighter*, p. 103; Hardy, p. 15.
14. *Junction City Union*, July 31, 1869.
15. Ibid.; *Kansas Historical Quarterly*, Vol. 26, 1960, p. 424.
16. Burkey, p. 5.
17. Ibid., p. 6.
18. Ibid., p. 6.
19. C. W. Miller, Pioneer, "Gives Impressions of the Days When Hays was Frontier Town," Hays *Daily News*, June 20, 1931; quoted in Burkey, p. 6.
20. Miguel Otero, *My Life on the Frontier 1864–1882*, New York, 1935, p. 14; quoted in Burkey, p. 6.
21. Hardy, p. 15.
22. C.W. Miller, loc. cit.
23. *Kansas City Journal of Commerce*, August 25, 1869; quoted in Burkey, p. 6.
24. Otero, p. 16; quoted in Burkey, p. 7.
25. Burkey, p. 7.
26. Joseph Hutt, "Sees 'Wild Bill' Make Crack Shots," *Ellis County News*, November 5, 1925; quoted in Burkey, p. 7.
27. Cal J. Bascom, "Wild Bill Days in Kansas," *Kansas City Star*, June 15, 1913; quoted in Burkey, p. 7.
28. Otero, p. 14; quoted in Burkey, p. 7.
29. Webb, pp. 145–148.
30. Burkey, p. 10.
31. Leavenworth *Times and Conservative*, September 28, 1869.
32. Leavenworth *Daily Commercial*, October 3, 1869.
33. Leavenworth *Daily Commercial*, n.d.; quoted by Lawrence *Daily Tribune*, September 30, 1869.
34. North Topeka *Times*, August 11, 1876.
35. Burkey, pp. 13–15. Burkey has an actual copy of the governor's letter to Gibson.
36. Ibid., p. 16.

37. "Recollections of John Ryan," *Circuit*, Newton, MA, September 3, 1909; quoted in Rosa, *They Called Him Wild Bill*, pp. 116–120.

## Chapter 7: In Old Abilene

1. McCoy, p. 44.
2. *Kansas Historical Quarterly*, Vol. IX 1940, pp. 242, 243. Biblical quote is from Luke 3:1.
3. Ibid.
4. Ibid., p. 244.
5. Ibid.
6. Ibid., p. 247.
7. Ibid., p. 248.
8. Ibid, pp. 249–250.
9. Ibid., p. 252.
10. Ibid., p. 253.
11. Ibid., p. 255
12. Ibid., p. 253; Rosa, *Gunfighter*, p. 140.
13. Ibid., p. 254.
14. *Kansas Historical Quarterly*, Vol. 26, 1960, p. 429.
15. Ibid., p. 430.
16. *Kansas Historical Quarterly*, Vol. IX, 1940, p. 255.
17. Abilene *Chronicle*, October 12, 1871.
18. *Junction City Union*, October 7, 1871.
19. Rosa, *They Called Him Wild Bill*, pp. 139–140; Time-Life The Old West, *The Gunfighters*, p. 39.
20. *The Gunfighters*, p. 180.
21. Abilene *Chronicle*, November 30, 1871.
22. *Kansas Historical Quarterly*, Vol. IX, 1940, p. 257.
23. Ibid.
24. Gil Robinson, *Old Wagon Show Days*, Cincinnati, OH, 1925, reprint, Literary Licensing LLC, 2013, p. 127.
25. Ibid., pp. 127–130.
26. Hardy, p. 18
27. Charles Gross to J. B. Edwards, April 13, 1922, and June 15, 1925; quoted in Rosa, p. 167.

## Chapter 8: Glory Days

1. Rosa, *They Called Him Wild Bill*, p. 173.
2. Buel, p. 416.
3. Buel, p. 417.
4. Buel, p. 157.
5. Ibid., pp. 157–158, 160–161.
6. Rosa, *Gunfighter*, p. 179.

7. Buel, pp. 158–159.
8. Ibid., p. 160.
9. Ibid., pp. 160–161.
10. Ibid., p. 163.
11. Rochester *Democrat and Chronicle*, March 14, 1874; quoted in Rosa, *Gunfighter*, pp. 184–185.
12. Buel, p. 163.
13. Ibid., pp. 162–163.
14. Ibid., pp. 163–164.
15. Story from Hiram Robbins related in Rosa, *Gunfighter*, p. 182.
16. Rosa, *Gunfighter*, p. 191.

## CHAPTER 9: SUNSET

1. Buel, pp. 167–168.
2. Ibid., pp. 168–169.
3. Raymond Thorp, *Spirit Gun of the West—The Story of Doc Carver*, Glendale, CA, 1957, reprint, Literary Licensing LLC, 2011, p. 244.
4. Cheyenne *Daily Leader*, August 16, 1876; quoted in Rosa, *Gunfighter*, pp. 194–195.
5. Annie Tallent, *The Black Hills, Or Last Hunting Grounds of the Dakotas*, St. Louis, MO, 1899, reprint, Brevet Press, Sioux Falls, SD, 1974, p. 100. Tallent was an early South Dakota pioneer in the Black Hills, and several landmarks were initially named for her. However, her obdurate attitude against Indians did not play well with later episodes of political correctness, and the landmarks that had her name subsequently removed it as a concession to Native American sensibilities.
6. Cheyenne *Daily Leader*, March 7, 1876.

## CHAPTER 10: THE BLACK HILLS

1. Buel, pp. 172–180.
2. Inscription from Thoen Stone, quoted in McClintock, p. 9.
3. Judge Horatio N. Maguire, *The Coming Empire*, 1878; quoted in McClintock, pp. 13–16.
4. Article by Dr. Cleophas O'Hara, *Black Hills Engineer*, November 1929; quoted in McClintock, p. 20.
5. Newspaper letters by William Curtis, Chicago *Inter-Ocean*, July 27 and August 3, 1874; quoted in McClintock, pp. 20, 21.
6. *South Dakota and Western Advocate*, October 15 1901; quoted in McClintock, p. 21.
7. Ibid., p. 30.
8. Ibid., pp. 32–33.
9. Ibid., p. 66.
10. Ibid., p. 69.
11. Many well-known Westerners married prostitutes, including at least one of the famed Earps.
12. Estelline Bennett, *Old Deadwood Days*, J. H. Sears and Co., New York, 1928, p. 6.
13. Ibid., p. 7.

14. Ibid., p. 8.

15. Ibid., p. 27.

16. Ibid., p. 29.

17. *The Life and Adventures of Calamity Jane*, circa 1894–1895(?); quoted in Don Clowser, *Deadwood-The Historic City*, Fenwyn Press, 1969, pp. 70–71.

18. Ibid., pp. 70–71.

19. Ibid., p. 71.

20. Ibid., p. 72.

21. Calamity Jane may, in fact, have married a cousin of Wild Bill with the same name, James Butler Hickok. A woman named Jean Hickok McCormick maintained that she was the daughter of Calamity Jane and Wild Bill Hickok's cousin, and she produced a series of documents that she claimed were her mother's diary for a newspaper story. Later, however, a changed version of the diary was presented and a previously unknown wedding certificate appeared, stating that Calamity Jane had in reality married the real Wild Bill Hickok, not his cousin. This all seems to be a fabrication. McCormick passed in and out of the public eye until her death in 1951, before which she harvested her fame as the "daughter of Wild Bill and Calamity Jane."

22. Letter from White Eye Anderson to Raymond Thorp, 1941; quoted in Rosa, *They Called Him Wild Bill*, p. 163.

23. Rosa, *They Called Him Wild Bill*, p. 164.

24. Letter from Wild Bill to Agnes Lake, Deadwood, SD, July 17, 1876; quoted in Buel, p. 188.

25. Like so much else about Wild Bill and many of these early Western figures, recent scholarship has shown that the photo does not, in fact, portray Utter. We have no accurate photographic representation of him.

26. *Daily Miner's Register*, June 28, 1865; quoted in John Koster, "The Man Who Wrote Wild Bill's Epitaph," *Wild West*, April 2015, Vol. 27, No. 6.

27. *Daily Miner's Register*, July 1865; quoted in Koster, p. 60.

28. *Rocky Mountain News*, May 9, 1866; quoted in Koster, p. 60.

29. Koster, pp. 60–61.

30. Dr. Junius E. Wharton, quoted in *The Rocky Mountain News*, May 1867; quoted in Koster p. 61.

31. Koster, pp. 61–62.

32. Koster, pp. 62–63.

33. John Hunton, *John Hunton's Diary*, Vol. II (1876–1877), edited by L. G. Flannery, Lingle, WY, 1956–1960, pp. 115–116; quoted in Rosa, *They Called Him Wild Bill*, p. 205.

34. Harry Young, quoted in Wilstach, *Wild Bill Hickok*, pp. 271–272.

35. Correspondence between White Eye Anderson to Raymond Thorp; quoted in Rosa, *They Called Him Wild Bill*, pp. 203–204.

36. White Eye Anderson to Raymond Thorp, quoted in Rosa, *They Called Him Wild Bill*, pp. 207–208.

37. Frank Wilstach, *Wild Bill Hickok*, Garden City Publishing, Garden City, NY, 1926, pp. 274–275; Rosa, *They Called Him Wild Bill*, pp. 210–211.

38. Wilstach, pp. 277–278.

39. Ibid., pp. 279–280.

40. Ibid., quoted Rosa, *They Called Him Wild Bill*, p. 281.
41. J. B. Hickok to wife, August 1, 1876; quoted in Wilstach, *Wild Bill Hickok*, p. 282.
42. Article in Cheyenne *Daily Leader*, August 26, 1876; quoted in Rosa, *Alias*, p. 213.
43. Richardson, p. 3.

## CHAPTER 11: TRIALS AND CONSEQUENCES

1. Rosa, *They Called Him Wild Bill*, pp. 214–215.
2. Joseph Rosa, *Alias Jack McCall*, Kansas City Posse of the Westerners, Kansas City, MO, 1967, p. 3.
3. Article from Chicago *Inter-Ocean*, August 17, 1876; quoted in Rosa, *They Called Him Wild Bill*, p. 217.
4. Letter from Doc Pierce, quoted in Wilstach, pp. 283–284.
5. Ibid., p. 285.
6. Correspondence between White Eye Anderson and Raymond Thorp, quoted in Rosa, *They Called Him Wild Bill*, p. 218.
7. Chicago *Inter-Ocean* newspaper story August 17, 1876, quoted in Rosa, *They Called Him Wild Bill*, p. 219.
8. Notice by Charlie Utter, August 2, 1876, quoted in Rosa, *They Called Him Wild Bill*, p. 219.
9. W. L. Kuykendall, *Frontier Days*, 1917, NP, pp. 187–189.
10. Buel, pp. 193–194.
11. Ibid., pp. 194–195.
12. Chicago *Inter-Ocean*, August 17, 1876; quoted in Rosa, *They Called Him Wild Bill*, pp. 228–229.
13. Ibid.
14. Buel, pp. 195–197; herein are the court statements from McCall's trial in Deadwood.
15. Ibid., pp. 197–198.

## CHAPTER 12: AFTERMATH

1. Cheyenne *Daily Leader*, August 26, 1876; quoted in Rosa, *They Called Him Wild Bill*, p. 232.
2. Article from Chicago *Record*, December 26, 1896; quoted in Rosa, *They Called Him Wild Bill*, pp. 223–224.
3. McClintock, p. 111.
4. Laramie Wyoming *Daily Leader*, August 30, 1876; quoted in Rosa, *They Called Him Wild Bill*, pp. 233–234.
5. Stories in, respectively, Cheyenne *Daily Leader*, September 1, 1876; August 30; September 1.
6. Rosa, *Alias*, pp. 5–6. This small, limited publication book (only 250 autographed copies were released) is a collection of official court documents Rosa obtained from the Federal Records Center in Kansas City, Missouri, and also from local newspapers, principally the *Yankton Daily Press and Dakotan*, still in existence today. Other biographies of Hickok, including Rosa's own *They Called Him Wild Bill*, did not have these

documents for their perusal. I am indebted to the excellent Western collection at the University of South Dakota ID Weeks Library for the use of this little known volume.

7. Buel, p. 191.

8. Rosa, *Alias*, pp. 8–9.

9. Ibid., p. 9.

10. Ibid., p. 9.

11. Rosa, *Gunfighter*; Richardson quoted in the *Pioneer Press*, September 8, 1876, p. 164.

12. Yankton *Daily Press and Dakotan* (hereafter referred to as the *P&D*), December 5, 1876; quoted in Rosa, *Alias Jack McCall*, p. 11.

13. Ibid.

14. *P&D*, December 5, 1876; quoted in Rosa, *Alias*, p. 13.

15. Ibid., quoted in Rosa, *Alias*, pp. 13–14.

16. *P&D*, December 5, 1876; quoted in Rosa, *Alias*, p. 14.

17. Rosa, *Alias*, p. 15.

18. *P&D*, December 6, 1876; quoted in Rosa, *Alias*, pp. 15–16.

19. Ibid.

20. Court Record Book, Second Judicial Court, Territory of Dakota, pp. 245–246; quoted in Rosa, *Alias*, pp. 16–17.

21. Ibid., pp. 245–246; quoted in Rosa, *Alias*, p. 17.

22. Ibid., p. 247; quoted in Rosa, *Alias*, p. 17.

23. Rosa, *Alias*, notes on footnote #44, p. 31.

24. *P&D*, December 7, 1876; quoted in Rosa, *Alias*, p. 18.

25. Court Record Book, p. 257; quoted in Rosa, *Alias*, p. 18.

26. Rosa, *Alias*, p. 19.

27. Reading obvious canards like this makes the author eternally grateful that he followed the advice of his mother and the urging of his own heart and dropped out of law school and instead earned a PhD in American history and became a teacher and writer, not an attorney.

28. Records of the Office of the Pardon Attorney, No. F-307, Records Group No. 204, National Archives, Washington DC; quoted in Rosa, *Alias*, p. 20.

29. Instead of mitigating their client's guilt, one would think this point would significantly exacerbate his guilt for a cold-blooded murder, with no aggravating circumstances to lessen his responsibility.

30. Ibid.; quoted in Rosa, *Alias*, pp. 21–22.

31. Rosa, *Alias*, p. 22.

32. These are very strong words for a federal prosecutor to use when one considers the kinds of murderers, thieves, and general dregs of society he had been used to seeing in his day-to-day work—apparently McCall was among the worst of the worst.

33. This is probably as close to a true motive as will ever be discovered for McCall's actions.

34. It is a mystery to the author why the State did not also charge McCall with attempted murder of bystanders as he tried to shoot his revolver at them but it failed to discharge, or even assault.

35. Records of the Pardon Attorney, No. F-307, Records Group No. 204, National Archives, Washington, DC; quoted in Rosa, *Alias*, pp. 22–24.

36. Ibid.; quoted in Rosa, *Alias*, p. 25.
37. Ibid.
38. *P&D*, February 28, 1877; quoted in Rosa, *Alias*, p. 26.
39. Rosa, *Alias*, p. 26.
40. Rosa, *Alias*, p. 26. Rosa asserted that Mary McCall was a housekeeper in a hotel in Louisville, Kentucky, from 1876–1877.
41. Rosa, *Alias*, pp. 26–28. The author's physician, Dr. William Dendinger, grew up in Yankton and told the author that as a small boy, the exact location of McCall's body was a frequent topic of conversation among Yankton residents.

## EPILOGUE: THE MYTH OF WILD BILL

1. Buel, p. 181.
2. Mari Sandoz, *The Buffalo Hunters*, New York, 1954, reprint, Bison Books, 1978, p. 259.
3. Cheyenne *Daily Leader*, August 3, 1880.
4. Ibid., July 19, 1881.
5. McClintock, pp. 112–113.

## APPENDIX: GUNS AND TECHNIQUES OF A LEGEND

1. Chris Kyle, *American Gun*, William Morrow, New York, 2013, pp. 59–65. Former Navy Seal sniper Chris Kyle and Wild Bill have several things in common. Both were deadly experts with firearms, both fearlessly faced death dozens of times, and both were killed by back-shooting cowards who tried to weasel out of their crimes.
2. Ibid., p. 74.
3. Rosa, *Gunfighter*, pp. 202–203.
4. Ibid., p.35.
5. Correspondence between Charles Gross and J. B. Edwards, Manuscripts Division, Kansas State Historical Society, Topeka, Kansas; quoted in Rosa, *Gunfighter*, pp. 57–59.
6. Chicago *Tribune*, August 25, 1876; quoted in Kyle, *American Gun*, p. 75.
7. Chauncey Thomas, "Interview with Bill Cody," *Outdoor Life*, January 10, 1917; quoted in Rosa, *Gunfighter*, p. 49.
8. Burlington, Iowa, *Daily Hawkeye*, January 29, 1886, interview with Bill Cody; quoted in Rosa, *Gunfighter*, pp. 49–50.

# Bibliography

## Newspapers Cited

Abilene *Chronicle*
Burlington, Iowa, *Daily Hawkeye*
Cheyenne *Daily Leader*
Chicago *Inter-Ocean*
Chicago *Record*
Chicago *Tribune*
Denver *Rocky Mountain News*
Hays *Daily News*
*Junction City Union*
Lawrence *Daily Tribune*
Leavenworth *Daily Commercial*
Leavenworth *Times and Conservative*
Missouri *Weekly Patriot*
North Topeka *Times*
Rochester *Democrat and Chronicle*
Topeka *Weekly Leader*
Yankton *Daily Press and Dakotaian*

## Books Cited and Consulted

Estelline Bennett, *Old Deadwood Days*, J. H. Sears, New York, 1928.
Levi Bloyd, *Rock Creek Station: The Scene of the Wild Bill/McCanles Killing*, no date or
    publisher given.
J. W. Buel, *Heroes of the Plains*, Standard Publishing Co., Philadelphia, 1886.
Blaine Burkey, *Wild Bill Hickok: The Law in Hays City*, by the author, Hays, Kansas, 1973.
Don Clowser, *Deadwood: The Historic City*, Fenwyn Press Books, 1969.
G. A. Custer, *My Life on the Plains*, Sheldon and Co., New York, 1874.
Charles Dawson, *Pioneer Tales of the Oregon Trail and Jefferson County Nebraska*, n.p.,
    Nebraska, 1912.
Daniel Dodge, *Lincoln's Inaugurals, Addresses and Letters*, Longmans, New York, 1910.
Mildred Fielder, *Wild Bill and Deadwood*, Superior Publishing Co., Seattle, 1965.
William Forbis, *The Cowboys*, The Old West: Time-Life Books, New York, 1973.

Allison Hardy, *Wild Bill Hickok: King of the Gunfighters*, Haldeman-Julius Publications, Girard, Kansas, 1943.

David Kennedy, *The American Pageant*, Vol. I-to 1877 (11th edition), Houghton Mifflin, Boston, 1998.

Irma Klock, *All Roads Lead to Deadwood*, by the author, Lead, SD, 1979.

W. L. Kuykendall, *Frontier Days*, 1917.

Chris Kyle, *American Gun*, William Morrow, New York, 2013.

John McClintock, *Pioneer Days in the Black Hills*, published by the author, Deadwood, SD, 1939.

Joseph McCoy, *Historic Sketches of the Cattle Trade of the West and Southwest*, Kansas City, MO, 1874. Reprint, University Nebraska Press, 1986.

Gil Robinson, *Old Wagon Show Days*, Cincinnati, OH, 1925. Reprint, Literary Licensing LLC, 2013.

Theodore Roosevelt, *Ranch Life and the Hunting Trail*, Century, New York, 1901.

Joseph Rosa, *Alias Jack McCall*, Lowell Press, Kansas City, MO, 1967.

———, *They Called Him Wild Bill*, University of Oklahoma Press, Norman, 1964.

———, *Wild Bill Hickok, Gunfighter*, University of Oklahoma Press, Norman, 2003.

Mari Sandoz, *The Buffalo Hunters*, New York, 1954. Reprint, Bison Books, 1978.

*Sketches from Lincoln—Inaugurations, Addresses, and Letters*, Longman, Green, and Co., New York, 1910.

Annie Tallent, *The Black Hills, Or Last Hunting Grounds of the Dakotas*, St. Louis, MO, 1899. Reprint, Brevet Press, Sioux Falls, SD, 1974.

Raymond Thorp, *Spirit Gun of the West—The Story of Doc Carver*, Glendale, CA, 1957. Reprint, Literary Licensing LLC, 2011.

Paul Trachtman, *The Gunfighters*, The Old West–Time-Life Books, New York, 1973.

Stanley Vestal, *Dodge City-Queen of the Cowtowns*, Harper Brothers, New York, 1952.

W.E. Webb, *Buffalo Land*, Hannaford and Co., Cincinnati and Chicago, 1872.

Frank Wilstach, *Wild Bill Hickok*, Garden City Publishing, Garden City, NY, 1926.

Robert Wright, *Dodge City-The Cowboy Capital*, Wichita, KS, 1913.

William H. Wright, *The Grizzly Bear*, Scribner, New York, 1913.

## HISTORICAL COLLECTIONS

Kansas State Historical Collections, Kansas State Historical Society, 1891–1896, Vol. V

Kansas State Historical Collections, Kansas State Historical Society, 1940, Vol. IX

Kansas State Historical Collections, Kansas State Historical Society, 1926–1928, Vol. XVII

Kansas State Historical Collections, Kansas State Historical Society, 1960, Vol. XXVI

## ARTICLES

Bob Boze Bell, "The Doomed Prince of the Pistoleers," *True West*, Vol. 63, Issue 11, November 2016.

R. K. DeArment, "No Sure Bet: Gambling on the Frontier," *Wild West*, Vol. 17, No. 6, April 2005.

Mary Franz, "The Real Men of Deadwood," *Wild West*, Vol. 19, No. 2, August 2006.

John Koster, "The Man Who Wrote Wild Bill's Epitaph," *Wild West*, Vol. 27, No. 6, April 2015.

Joseph Rosa, "Wild Bill Hickok: Pistoleer, Peace Officer and Folk Hero," *Wild West*, Vol. 15, No. 5, March 2003.

Stuart Lake, "Guns and Gunfighters," *The Saturday Evening Post*, Vol. CCIII, No. 18, November 1, 1930.

Robert Dykstra, "The Last Days of Texan Abilene: A Study in Community Conflict on the Far Frontier," *Agricultural History*, Vol. 34, No. 3, July 1960.

Gregory Lalire, "When Stagecoaches Rolled the West," *Wild West*, Vol. 14, No. 6, April 2002.

Leander Richardson, "A Trip to the Black Hills," *Scribner's Monthly*, Vol. XIII, February 1877.

Phil Spangenberger, "Fantastic Firearms in Cody: Wild Bill Hickok's 1851 Colt Navy," *True West*, Vol. 63, Issue 11, November 2016.

# Index

# About the Author

Dr. Aaron Robert Woodard holds a bachelor's and master's degree in American history and American government from the University of South Dakota, and a PhD in American history from Trinity Saint David College in the United Kingdom. He teaches history and government at University Center and Augustana University in Sioux Falls, South Dakota. He has taught at the collegiate level for fifteen years. He is also the author of *Soft Fur and Iron Men—A History of the Fur Trade in South Dakota and the Upper Missouri* (2006). He has been an editorial writer for the *Indianapolis News* and has written many articles for various peer-reviewed academic journals, including *Journal of the West*, *Overland Journal*, and *Heritage of the Great Plains*. His latest journal article was "Incidents of Lawlessness: Theodore Roosevelt Bags His Men" in the Winter 2016 issue of *Heritage of the Great Plains*.